THE MISSING PIECE

Also by Herm Card

The Poet Within
The Poetry of Teaching
…or else it's only a job.
Once Around and In

Also by Dolores Card

For Kendra: Who Rides the Whales and Lives Among the Stars

Herm and Dolores are also authors of numerous articles in magazines and professional journals in their respective fields.

THE MISSING PIECE

educating new kids for a new world

DOLORES R. CARD, HERMON R. CARD

BALBOA PRESS
A DIVISION OF HAY HOUSE

Copyright © 2013 Dolores R. Card, Hermon R. Card.

All rights reserved. No part of this book may be used or reproduced by any means, graphic, electronic, or mechanical, including photocopying, recording, taping or by any information storage retrieval system without the written permission of the publisher except in the case of brief quotations embodied in critical articles and reviews.

Balboa Press books may be ordered through booksellers or by contacting:

Balboa Press
A Division of Hay House
1663 Liberty Drive
Bloomington, IN 47403
www.balboapress.com
1-(877) 407-4847

Because of the dynamic nature of the Internet, any web addresses or links contained in this book may have changed since publication and may no longer be valid. The views expressed in this work are solely those of the author and do not necessarily reflect the views of the publisher, and the publisher hereby disclaims any responsibility for them.

The author of this book does not dispense medical advice or prescribe the use of any technique as a form of treatment for physical, emotional, or medical problems without the advice of a physician, either directly or indirectly. The intent of the author is only to offer information of a general nature to help you in your quest for emotional and spiritual well-being. In the event you use any of the information in this book for yourself, which is your constitutional right, the author and the publisher assume no responsibility for your actions.

Any people depicted in stock imagery provided by Thinkstock are models, and such images are being used for illustrative purposes only. Certain stock imagery © Thinkstock.

Printed in the United States of America.

ISBN: 978-1-4525-7726-5 (sc)
ISBN: 978-1-4525-7728-9 (hc)
ISBN: 978-1-4525-7727-2 (e)

Library of Congress Control Number: 2013911685

Balboa Press rev. date: 08/01/2013

OUR BOOK IS DEDICATED TO
KENDRA MCPEAK 1985-1997

The first new kid of our family's current generation, your short stay with us taught us life's most important lesson—unconditional love.

Whose life was not changed by knowing you?
We are ever grateful.

April 22, 1985

CHILD OF THE UNIVERSE

*The flutter of tiny wings, so soft,
inaudible, except in our hearts.
for one ethereal moment,
the universe paused...*

*the angels whispered that you were here.
There was a hush as you
settled into our midst;*

*a lighted being who touched down
on earth to gather human energy.*

**The keynote of this child will be heard
by those willing to listen.**

For Kendra: Who Rides the Whales and Lives Among the Stars
Dolores Card, 1997

What nobler employment, or more valuable to the state, than that of the one who instructs the rising generation.

Marcus Tullius Cicero
De Divinatione, II, circa 78 BCE

CONTENTS

INTRODUCTION XV

SECTION ONE

Chapter One   *The New Kids: who are they?* 3

Chapter Two   *The Journey of Humanity: the New Kids through the ages.* . 27

Chapter Three   *The Missing Piece: our spiritual nature; the nature of our spirituality.* 35

SECTION TWO

Chapter Four   *The Art of Teaching* 51

Chapter Five   *The Act of Teaching: activities and applications* 85

Chapter Six   *New and Selected Poetry from The Poetry of Teaching and ...or else it's only a job..* 137

SECTION THREE

Introduction to Metaphysics: Beyond the Five Senses 161

Chapter Seven   *The Wonderful World of Metaphysics:* 165

Chapter Eight   *New Age Movement: not so new.* 171

Chapter Nine   *The Sound of Silence: the comfort and power of meditation.* . 179

Chapter Ten   *The Higher Self: get acquainted with the real you* 189

Chapter Eleven   *The Courage To Be You: connecting with your power of courage* 193

Chapter Twelve   *A Bit about Chakras: why the New Kids need to know about them* 197

Chapter Thirteen   *Reiki: The Ancient Healing Art.* 207

SECTION FOUR

Chapter Fourteen *Alternative Education* 219

Chapter Fifteen *Echoes and Reflections: voices of students and teachers*. . . . 233

Ending Thoughts... 239

Endnotes 243

Bibliography/Recommended Reading. 247

The Authors 249

The Authors 251

We have written *The Missing Piece* based on our shared expertise and personal experiences in our respective fields. It reflects our passion for making education, and the people we educate, better.

Our diverse, yet similar backgrounds allow us to speak to you in different voices but in the common language of commitment to students, teachers, and the future they will create.

Herm and Dolores Card

To the world's children and to those yet to be born: *Thank you for your courage to be here, for the many gifts that you bring and your insight for a new world.*

To the new kids of our family:
Kendra McPeak, Erinn McPeak, Ryan McPeak, Katheryn Rothenberg, Alexandria Chappell, Chris Chappell, Kevin McPeak, Rebecca Rothenberg, Sierra McPeak, Brandon McPeak
You have brought much joy into our lives and you have taught us how to be. We often forget our playfulness, what it was like to climb trees, run around for no reason and jump in mud puddles—thank you for reminding us.

To our previous generation of new kids:
Don McPeak, Vanessa McPeak, David McPeak, Dawn McPeak, Jean Card, Stuart Moll, Stefanie Rothenberg, Glen Rothenberg, Chris Mahar McPeak
Thank you for being who you are.

This project could not have been completed without the support of family, friends and advisors. A special thank you to each of you for being our companions on this long, over-due and sometimes exhausting journey, that allows us to bring to light the birthright of all children to be given a comprehensive education.

To all who endured interviews, long discussions and gave their time and attention to our subject; who reviewed, suggested, offered insight and validation; who took the time to listen and still count us as family and friends; and Ron Trinca for using his creative talents to design our cover:

THANK YOU!

Planned Obsolescence

Things with warranties
are designed to fail;
light bulbs, mowers, cars, TVs.

Things without warranties
are not designed to fail;
rivers, mountains, trees, children.

...or else it's only a job.
Herm Card, 2006

INTRODUCTION

There is always a door that opens in childhood to let the future in.
Barton Gregorian

We Are In The Midst of an Education Crisis.

Education, in its broadest sense, is the means through which patterns and beliefs of a collective group sustains from one generation to the next. The Etymology of the word "education" is derived from the Latin word *educatio*: a breeding, a bringing up, a rearing.

Education can form the way we think, feel and behave. It helps to establish our ethics and our perspective of the world. We continue to pass our knowledge, skills and customs as well as our societal and family values to each succeeding generation, in large part, through instructions in school. How often do we assess if what we are forwarding on to the next generation is what is needed in conjunction with changing trends and advances we become aware of?

To merely pass on our own standards and attitudes can result in impeding and delaying social and economic changes needed. It is our responsibility to not make clones of ourselves to feed our egos, but to try to anticipate the obligations of future generations. While it is not wrong to project some of the qualities that we have deemed positive for creating a purposeful life, we must allow for adjustment of these values as they fit into future circumstances. "Our way, or no way" does not work.

When examining the purpose of schools, which includes developing reasoning, mastering methods of scientific exploration and cultivating the intellect, the primary purpose is to teach students how to think. Not teaching them a certain *way* or *what* to think, but to use their thinking as a method to reach conclusions about their life experiences, first about their individual world and then to extend their thinking to global issues.

We are failing to recognize that the past two generations are wired differently. They do not relate to the "one size fits all" model. We are failing them by forcing them to fit into an education approach that no longer works. These are young people of technology and purpose. We are neglecting to provide them with the tools to become the individuals they need to be in order to reach their full potential.

Every twenty years or so, "new" ways of learning are introduced, but they invariably fail to address the multi-layered needs of the children. New concepts are mostly based on numbers and accomplishments of school districts that need to measure up to standards set by state and national directives. We have lost the human element in teaching, which is what these exceptional students need the most.

There is an education revolution in progress. These new kind of students will not tolerate being forced into doing much of anything, most of all a system that does not encourage their creativity and unique personal expression. They are much too bright and aware to allow suppression of their own methods of thinking and reaching conclusions. If pushed, they will opt out, many already have. Data for 2010-2011shows that 26 states reported lower graduation rates with at least seven states reporting a double digit decline.

Current developers of education mandates have not accepted the truth of who we are as a human race or as individuals, both in our innate talents and capabilities. The roots of curriculum refer to the course of expression through which children become mature adults. Curricula are based on a general syllabus which specifies what topics must be understood and to what level to achieve a particular grade or standard. When did we last look at the topics to determine what would be most beneficial to build life skills in addition to pertinent information for each subject?

Current education laws and mandates have not been adjusted to the changing characteristics of present day students. We must be willing to revise, and in some instances, discard current curricula being imposed upon these new thinkers or the battle for meaningful education will never be won. If we are to pass the baton to this generation, we must make sure that we have a solid foundation to pass to them to help prepare them for the demands that lie ahead.

There is a prevailing fear that permeates the human race that to deviate from what has been established will result in chaotic failure. "If it ain't broke, don't fix it" philosophy does not allow for assessment of current practices and how effective they still are. To blindly trust that a system is still working is a recipe for disaster. If our ancestors believed that eating raw meat was the only way to go, the discovery of fire would have only served to keep them warm.

The human race is moving forward in ways never before experienced. A new way of life is dawning on this planet. If we are to benefit from these changes, we must attend to those beautiful young people who are sitting in our classrooms, as this opportunity will not come again.

The following pages will offer, through philosophies, poetry and practical applications, insight into building a better world by empowering our children with the resources, life skills and self confidence that can only be endowed to them through effective education.

SECTION ONE

THE NEW KIDS: *who are they?*

THE JOURNEY OF HUMANITY: *the new kids through the ages*

THE MISSING PIECE

Times Have Changed

When I was in eighth grade
I wrote of
baseball
and Christmas
and summer
and family
and fun
and other stuff that eighth graders knew.

My students in eighth grade
write of
abuse
and poverty
and crime
and divorce
and suicide
and terrorism
and other stuff that eighth graders know.
The Poetry of Teaching
Herm Card, 1998

CHAPTER ONE

I am...I said
Neil Diamond

THE NEW KIDS: *who are they?*

Teachers, there are new kinds of students in your classrooms, who:

- display wisdom beyond their years with expressions of intelligence that cannot be measured by standardized tests.
- have the ability to reach correct conclusions, without knowing the process of how they arrived at the answer and are not interested in learning what the process is.
- are very independent and prefer to discover information on their own.
- are extremely gifted in one or more areas, many have an amazing natural talent for music.
- are oriented towards science more than any other subject.
- learn quickly even though they do not think sequentially and process information in unusual ways.
- display abstract thinking, which they learned to do at an early age and communicate in multiple ways.
- feel that they know a better way of doing things and do not respond well to being told that "it has always been done this way."
- can be disruptive and restless and may act like what you are trying to teach them is completely irrelevant to them.
- cause educators to rethink old standards of teaching and why they are not working with these students.

- score high IQ scores, even when failing a subject or even a grade level.
- exasperate you and puzzle you, but cause you to be amazed at their insight[1].

Recognize them?

Who are They?

Some have labeled them Indigo children, Crystal children and Psychic children, none of which totally represent who they really are. We have also put other labels on them like ADD, ADHD, ED, LD, AUTISTIC, etc., which misrepresents some of them in a more profound way.

We prefer to call them the new kids. They have brought with them not only a new vigor, but a concentrated focus to help the human race to evolve into new depth of awareness. Those born since the early 1980s, have occupied desks in your classrooms, messy (or neat) bedrooms in your homes, played on athletic fields and filled the hallways at school, as well as your hearts and homes, with a distinctive kind of energy. They sit in classrooms looking at you through disinterested eyes and somehow know they have been compelled by law to absorb as much information as their brains will hold to be able to bring up their test scores to satisfy standards. These test scores primarily are used to maintain the myth that students can be evaluated literally. Often, through frustration, they begin to exhibit behaviors that cause concern for teachers and administrators, not to mention their parents.

We apologize for applying the term "kids" to those who have already reached adulthood, those who were the forerunners for the present generation. 30 plus years ago you were the new kids and since then have added your contributions to the needed changes in our human community. The greatest contribution for some of you is being the parents of the most recent generation of new kids. Many of you have already entered into the teaching profession and are among those who are struggling with worn out, ineffective methods of education.

The Missing Piece

How Do We Reach Them, Raise Them and Educate Them?

They have arrived on Earth with an instinctive mission to challenge patterns and beliefs that have become counter-productive, even harmful to the qualities needed by the period of time in which we live; an overhaul of society. They are building the bridge to better ways of being.

The goal of this book is to show, through concrete scientific facts, concepts, theories and beliefs based on metaphysical studies, how and why these young people no longer fit into our perceptions of students.

Educating the New Kids: developing a complete human being

No matter what their present personal beliefs are or where they stand on their spiritual nature, educators cannot deny the emergence of a different kind of student. Science has slowly but consistently opened to the idea of what we might consider a new "type" of human being.

Evolution moves forward with regularity to be compatible with the requirements of each generation. We are accelerating our progress as a species and the effects of this can clearly be seen in our youngest citizens—our current students.

Some important studies have been introduced, which will be cited in this book. We need to adjust our fear of change and social disapproval to cultivate an education system that teaches to every aspect of a student. We have much to learn from our failed efforts, in order to create more effective methods of teaching.

New kids do not fit the typical descriptions of a student. They feel that most instruction is beneath their level of reasoning and will resist listening to lectures about topics they feel are not relevant to their life. They will become bored and restless, lose interest and tune you out.

They are children of the moment and are interested in hearing information that will help them move forward in the direction of their purpose.

What is missing and often dismissed is information about the evolution of human consciousness that has been brought down through the ages through oral histories, storytelling and customs that depict changes in human insight and awareness. If we listen closely to these accounts from the people who observed the day to day changes in themselves and others, we can clearly trace the discovery of our inner nature.

IQ test scores of students in the United States have risen significantly, as well as in other countries. Many current students display an intelligence that far exceeds that of previous generations.

In contrast, many teachers and school psychologists report that they are seeing just the opposite in regard to IQ scores. They also observe that a high percentage of students appear to be disinterested in what their school has to offer. Many are unable to achieve any significant academic success and give the impression that they don't care to be successful. For some, attendance at school is sporadic, at best.

Are these the same kids that we have been talking about? Yes, some are the same kids, but those whose life circumstances have failed to recognize and nurture their exceptional character traits. The reality is that their potential is not being addressed, resulting in them falling further into the abyss of negative thinking and risky behavior.

It must be remembered that they see the world through different eyes. They are new people with a different perspective. They are very creative and very sensitive. Therefore a lack of attention to their need for understanding affects them deeply, making it difficult for them to follow their inner feelings of wanting to accomplish something meaningful. Some of these students have rejected their sense of worth and are buying into the stereotype of the "difficult student". To many of them it seems pointless to try to correct this impression.

IQ scores do not reflect the intelligence potential of these students or the way their minds work. Because they perceive reality differently, the information we are trying to impart to them can cause confusion. Scores may be declining, but their intelligence is not.

The Language of Their Passion

Finding where students' passions lie is not that difficult. Passion and talents often correspond. They will gravitate towards their areas of attraction and look for opportunities to participate in or talk about their favorite activities. They will also be more successful in these areas. As the interest develops, and there is no discouragement, it may become a path to a future career.

It is almost impossible to fully predict potential, but helping a student to identify what is important to them is a good place to start. What a person enjoys speaks to something on an inner level. It may be filling a void left by a loss or traumatic event or it might be that it simply reflects the true nature of that person. Being encouraged to talk about an interest will instill confidence by allowing a student to display knowledge and talents about the subject and can create a feeling of belonging. It may also be an opportunity to connect to others who have the same interests and inner goals, which can lessen their feelings of isolation. It is very important for this generation to connect and interact with like-minded people to validate what excites and motivates them.

As they become more comfortable sharing what is important to them, a common language emerges that helps to solidify connections to others and many times cultivates friendships. Expanding their peer group and community connections can also help kids to advance beyond a dysfunctional environment and be motivated to make good choices.

The simple activity that follows has proven to be helpful in opening up communication with peers, without the fear of judgment. It also offers students an opportunity to practice how to effectively express their thoughts.

- Give students a few minutes to think of something that interests them. It can be a hobby, an academic subject or an area of expertise.
- In pairs, each student explains that interest to the other.
- Each listener tells his/her partner what they learned about the exchange.
- Teachers may determine an appropriate culminating activity.

Dolores R. Card, Hermon R. Card

Teachers affect eternity;
but one can never tell where their influence stops.
Henry Brooks Adams

Planting Seeds of Thought

The analogy of planting seeds in a garden and planting seeds in the human mind is clear. A seed of a certain flower or vegetable is carefully imbedded in the soil of the Earth. Nature recognizes what is to be grown and begins its' course. However, to grow the best flowers or vegetables, nurturing of the seeds is needed to help nature to succeed. Water, nutrients and sunlight encourage growth.

The developing human brain also needs nourishing in much the same way. In order to teach a child a concept that they view as something useful to them, we need to nurture those thoughts, by encouraging exploration of the subject matter over a period of time. Presenting material on a one time basis is not nurturing. Examining the point of the lesson in various situations helps new kids to accept that what you are telling them somehow relates to their lives. The gifts that we bring to life will blossom with attention; the rewards are continuing opportunities to grow.

The truth is that it may not be important that each student thoroughly understands the information you are trying to teach them at the time. (a radical statement) If you plant the right seeds, they may not germinate until needed. It could be two days, two months or it could be fifteen years later: "Oh, that's what he/she was talking about."

We use information when required by our life circumstances, so what may have been in that lesson, or on that exam, although it did not register then, is rising up in memory to meet that need. Test scores reflect this phenomenon. At the time of the test to know the correct answers to the questions may reflect what is important or *not* important to that student's life at that moment. That is how the new kids' brains work. Outcomes of standardized tests do not reflect the importance of that information to that particular student, nor does it reflect their capabilities.

Multiple intelligences

In 1998 Dr. Howard Gardner expanded the theory of multiple intelligences.[2] Since IQ tests mostly measure logical-mathematical and linguistic intelligence, he recommended that teachers present material in a variety of ways to accommodate the different learning styles of students.

One of the consequences of not measuring other forms of intelligence is that students have sometimes been labeled as having learning disabilities because their particular way of learning was not an option.

Students learn, remember, perform and understand in different ways. These differences challenge an education system that assumes that everyone can learn the same material in the same way and that a universal measurement suffices to test students' learning. The following is an adaptation of Gardner's theory from www.literacyworks.org,[3] as well as adaptations of our own.

INTELLIGENCE	DESCRIPTION	HOW TO ENGAGE
Language (linguistic)	sensitive to language, meanings, and the relationship of words	vocabulary activities, poetry, essays, plays, personal journals
Spatial	keen observer, three dimensional, good with metaphors	graphs, charts, color code guides, imagery, pictures, posters, mind maps
Logic/math	abstract thinking, counting organizing, prefers logical structures	critical thinking activities, analyzing word structure, geometry
Body Movement (kinesthetic)	good body control and fine motor skills, active and animated	hands-on learning opportunities, like games, skits, plays, sports
Musical	sensitive to rhythm, pitch, intonation and can remember tunes and rhythms easily	poetry, plays, jazz chants, rap music, songs musically guided imagery
Social (interpersonal)	sensitive to others' moods feelings and motivations; outgoing and sensitive	discussion groups, debates, problem solving activities
Self (intrapersonal)	has sense of self, able to access and understand one's own feelings	poetry, meditations, guided imagery, journal; writing and story telling
Nature (naturalist)	sensitive to nature and environment, knows names of rocks and flowers, loves to be outdoors	garden work, studying fish and birds, hiking and camping, environmental causes, connection to animals

The theory of multiple intelligences is very important to education on several levels. First, it encourages teachers and administrators to recognize the different intelligences among students. That trying to educate with a curriculum that is one dimensional does not work. Period. Offering lessons that have multiple intelligences content give options to students to learn by applying their own learning style. This way of instruction can result in more successful outcomes for both teacher and student, something that both are striving for. Making it possible for students to learn in their own way, opens up the possibility for them to become energized about their education. Again, it is a two-way street. As students respond positively, teachers can re-capture their self-confidence and enthusiasm for teaching.

Maybe without realizing it, Dr. Gardner was laying the groundwork for educating the new kids. If you examine each of the types of intelligence, it becomes obvious that each absolutely fits the characteristics of these exceptional students and in many cases, their teachers.

Engaging the New Kids: teachers and students do not have separate agendas—they are co-participants in the process of education.

Creative and innovative ways to engage and employ the innate intelligence and analytical thinking skills of the new kids are essential if we are to reap the benefits of their new patterns of influence and intentions, not to mention hanging on to them long enough for them to complete their education.

The following are general suggestions to support and enhance the education of the new kids. Useful, effective activities follow in later chapters. A partnership must be formed with the new kids to give them a sense of being included in decisions made about their learning. It also fosters a greater opportunity for them to invest in their own education. It would also serve to build trust between student and teacher. Working with these students is, at best, frustrating; but can also be exciting if teachers consider their students' perspective as part of this partnership. To enlist their help is a big step to gain confidence in the teachers' approach.

The key? Discover *how* they want to learn. A good place to start is at the beginning of a new school year. Explain what you need to accomplish. Be honest; they will know if you are trying to merely placate them. Explain, in terms appropriate for the grade level, what you need to accomplish in a definite time frame. Talk with them about what they need to learn and discuss ways to reach these objectives together. They need to know that some things cannot be changed, but ask for their input for ideas to achieve your shared goals.

- An example hand out to students might look like this:

Objective (goal)   Methods that could be used

_____

_____

_____

Allow younger students to experiment with ways to think about their projects to both further develop their critical thinking skills and learn to walk through the process and methods of completing their projects (Remember, the new kids are not very tolerant of learning this skill). Encourage them to show you their projects and describe how they did it. Critical thinking, or reflective thinking, is interpretation of information using reason in forming beliefs and making decisions.

Be very careful to not compare students or their work to each other. New kids will not allow even the suggestion that they take on others' abilities as their own. They will not react favorably, which is an understatement. It is one of the instances where they defend their uniqueness and individuality.

Give recognition and value to any efforts made to complete a project, whether it is a written assignment or a hands-on task, especially when the assignment was not completed. Discuss why it was not completed and give credit for the effort. There is not enough merit given to effort made. This does not apply, of course, to the student who just decides not to do the assignment; all students need to be accountable for their work.

The prevailing belief (not without merit) is that with all the mandates to be met by teachers, there is not enough time to include students having a say in their education.

The harsh reality is that if these students continue to try to learn under current methods, we will lose them somewhere along the way. They are here to change these very systems that need improvement and will not accept that we have to adhere to education principles simply because they have always been done that way.

Every student should discover their learning style. It can affirm their strong points and help avoid feeling deficient because the style in which the lesson was presented did not correspond with their skills. New kids are mostly spatial learners. Most traditional schooling methods are based on auditory, sequential learning. They will have high grades in subjects that correspond to their visual learning style, but lower grades in subjects that are presented in sequential order, like math; unless the math problem makes a connection to a real life situation. Because they think in pictures, they should be allowed to take notes in forms appropriate to their learning style, as written notes can be a real struggle for them.

New kids instinctively know their importance and need validation. A good activity in art class would be to either design a t-shirt on paper, or if feasible, to actually paint on a real t-shirt, a few words that describes their character. (appropriate language rule, of course) Designing on paper a few positive words for other class members, would help them with the process of being able to comfortably share thoughts with others, especially in a peer group. New kids like positive feedback on how others view them. It also gives them the opportunity to utilize their artistic creativity.

Receiving information passively or through lectures is not always productive. They need discussion, debate and open ended questions. They need to offer opinions and feel that they are not being judged because they are willing to speak about their beliefs. They need "wiggle room" with problems to solve and challenges to hone their critical thinking skills.

All students need physical education, music and art as an important part of their complete education. These programs are often the first to get cut from a school budget during a fiscal crisis. Both are a prerequisite if we are to teach to the whole child. Those that downplay the importance of physical education are not considering the advantages of a fit, healthy student. A child that can master physical tasks gains confidence and legitimate self-esteem, making them much more likely to engage in academic studies.

There is high correlation between music and math. Studies have shown that students who do well in music also excel in math.[4] Some research shows that starting music lessons at a young age enhances math ability. Pythagoras, known as the father of mathematics, found many correlations between math and music. Music theorists use math to understand and write music. Math is involved in every part of music from simple additions to complicated functions, including note lengths, measures, time signatures and frequencies of sound.

New kids are very connected to music. Whether it is playing an instrument, writing compositions or just listening to favorite songs, they must be given opportunities to be involved in music in some way.

Music is often called the universal language. Regardless of traditions or cultural differences, people are able to experience emotions through music. It has been interwoven in our lives and connects us in shared moments of celebration. Music affects our brain waves, our emotions, heart rate and breathing. It can excite us to joy or move us to tears.

Music therapy has become an application for helping people to cope with pain and depression and other types of health related issues. It is a most important form of communication with the new kids as well as a way to express what they cannot say in words. Music also acts as a way for them to cope with the stressors of life.

R.J., a 16-year-old student says, *I love the quote by an unknown author that says: "Music is what feelings sound like." The violin and piano act as my voice when I do not know the necessary words to use as communication. I believe that my compassionate and sensitive personality is the result of music and the calm it brings over me. When the weight of the world seems like it is on the top of my shoulders, music invokes my determination to push through any obstacle. The instruments I perform with are not just tools, but provide me with the ability to let go of my frustrations and free myself from reality.*

Health is Happiness and Happiness is Health

While some schools have incorporated this *most* crucial element, every unit on health in *every* school district should include a component about emotional health. Health classes should start at the elementary level before behaviors that are counterproductive to their well-being are firmly established.

The cause of all negative emotions is a disruption in the body's energy system. The human body is an electromagnetic organism and when a person is tuned into (thinking about) something negative it causes difficulty in our flow of energy. Creating an environment through activities that point out this phenomenon could enable a student to focus on school instead of being distracted by negative thinking of a personal nature.

Our subconscious is essentially neutral and like a computer, it will supply whatever we tell it to. There is so much power in our words. Our thoughts become reality through our words. As our thinking can create our mental and emotional state, the importance of using self-affirming language can serve to help stop the cycle of self-criticism. A negative self-concept can not only affect academic achievement, it is also detrimental to healthy relationships with others.

The following activities can encourage students to practice behaviors that will help them to achieve a balance of their emotions and live a healthier life.

ACTIVITY 1: *Tell Me Who You Are* (great for a health class, but could be done in other subjects)

The teacher explains how negative words can affect people's self-esteem, their ability to focus and their experience of school.

Each student is then assigned to write a paragraph describing him or herself and the teacher instructs them to:

- look for negative words they may have used in their description
- look for self-critical thoughts, images or feelings
- after a brief class discussion, reread their paragraph and look for words they may not have viewed as negative

The teacher and students then discuss how these words, thoughts, images or feelings could affect how people see themselves and how that can affect emotions. Have students suggest a more positive word to replace each negative one.

This activity can also be done by having the student or the teacher read the paragraph aloud, sharing with the other students. This would give the class a way to identify in their own writing or those of others, what they think are negative words and discuss why they think these words may be unkind or upsetting.

The activity can also be done over a period of time where the teacher reads the work privately and writes the words for the students to see that are, or seem negative, and share them with the class without naming the author of the writing.

ACTIVITY 2: *Ways to Positive Self-Concept* (ways to help students accept who they are)

Young people sometimes have a difficult time accepting that each person has characteristics unique to their personality that make them who they are. When the differences seem to set them apart from others, it can validate that they don't fit in or are unworthy of peer relationships. This is especially true for the new kids.

Completing the following sentences can encourage students to be introspective about their personality traits and come to accept that while they may differ from others, they are not necessarily negative or wrong. A healthy self-concept is the key to a rewarding life. Teachers can assign several sentences to complete or one at a time.

This activity would be best done a few weeks into the school year to give the students a chance to become acquainted with their classmates, which may make them more willing to share their answers.

"Even though I _____, I accept myself." It can be turned around to read: "I accept myself, even though I _____."

It is the teacher's discretion as to whether it is a onetime activity or used over a period of time. Whether the students share their answers with the class is *always* optional. (New kids love having choices).

These activities can be easily modified for a lesson about how using negative words can affect other people as well as themselves.

The Eraser

The soft felt of the eraser
caresses the blackboard
and gently whisks away
the soft chalk,
the white powder
drifting down like gentle snow,
no longer spelling
the awful things her friend had
written about her.

…or else it's only a job.
Herm Card 2006

It is important that teachers keep conversations with, and instructions to, students throughout the year in positive language. They can also listen for negative words that are being used by students and point them out and discuss them.

It's Not an Add-On, It's Essential

Starting out, as part of a daily routine, with meditation can help to ensure a more peaceful, less stressful and productive day for everyone. (see chapter nine, on meditation) The best practice for students would be to permit them a few minutes every morning to adjust to the school environment and begin to calmly focus on being open to receiving and understanding the lessons of the day. It does not have to be called meditation, it can be referred to as 'quiet time" or "time to prepare" or any other euphemism that is acceptable in a public school setting. There will come a day when meditation is incorporated into mainstream curriculum.

Giving students a few minutes to quiet their brains before tests will also help them concentrate on the material with less anxiety. (see short meditation in chapter nine).

As health classes have some latitude in subject matter, they would be an ideal place to begin to offer meditation in order to allow young people to experience the benefits first hand, which could become a lifelong healthful practice.

Labeling

If a child cannot sit down at a piano and innately know how to play, we don't call him/her learning disabled and prescribe medication. We teach the child how to play by giving lessons, time to practice and perhaps years to become accomplished. However, if that same child is having a problem learning to read and write or to do math, many times we call them learning disabled, which can lead to psychological difficulties, if the diagnosis is incorrect.

When a new kid is labeled ADHD, for instance, their inner feeling of being different is validated. Often it is not ADHD or ADD, but the nature of the new kid, creating selective attention to what *they* think is important. If a student can focus on a topic of their choice for long periods of time, it's probably not ADD. Even if there is a distraction or attention problem, medication is not always the answer and only after careful consideration and assessment of all the elements of the perceived problem. There are alternative methods of therapy that do not suppress their natural creativity and leadership traits. Overmedication can be devastating to a new kid, especially if given at a young age. Reliance on medication can set a pattern for disinterest and lack of motivation to be successful.

That is not to say that identifying students who need to receive support and help to rise to their potential is not indicated. Legitimate brain dysfunction needs to be addressed, but the assessment needs to go hand in hand with evaluation of the environment in which the child is developing. Some new kids, who have not been given the opportunities to develop their abilities and innate skills, will withdraw and some will inevitably show up as special education students.

In record numbers, elementary age new kids are being diagnosed as autistic, as it is not uncommon for them to have delayed speech patterns, often waiting until they are three or four years old to begin speaking. (Einstein, for example, didn't speak a word until the age of four). The true autistic person lives in an isolated world, disconnected from other people and doesn't talk because of an indifference to communicate with others. New kids, especially of elementary school age, are very communicative, caring and more people oriented than any previous generation. They love to care for people in need. An autistic person would not behave in this way.

A prevailing problem is the practice of administering traditional IQ tests to autistic children. It is well documented that students diagnosed with autism score poorly on traditional IQ tests. Psychologists have reported that when they adapted the test to exclude social interaction between the test giver and the student, the resulting scores were much higher.

A 2011 study at the University of Montreal[5] likewise concluded that administering non-verbal IQ tests to children with autism results in a significant rise in scores. This indicates that their true intelligence quotient is frequently going undiscovered. That oversight can result in the lifelong consequence of these children being labeled as low functioning or with lower than normal intelligence, even though that is not always the case.

A provocative statement from the study suggests that society has been biased in its view of autism and should accept the condition as one in which an individual presents unique characteristics. Dr. Mottron, conductor of the study, further states in his argument that we must stop considering the different brain structure of autistic individuals to be a deficiency as many autistics have qualities and abilities that exceed those of individuals without the condition.

In fact, news reports as recent as May, 2013 confirm this, saying that software companies in several countries have begun to employ people with autism as software testers and programmers. Employers praise their ability to focus on tasks for long periods of time and to spot minute discrepancies in data. Their unique skills have proven to be highly beneficial to product quality.

It is encouraging, and not surprising, that their skills with technology are finally being recognized.

New kids will not be disregarded. They will find a way to get your attention. They are excellent at crisis management; this is where their talents shine. As their physical senses are expanding they are becoming more alert to the world around them and better able to manage complex situations that confront them. It is our obligation to help them to develop this capability in positive ways.

A crucial ingredient for empowering our students is based on the fact that they are wired to become residents of the world. It is not enough for them to be able to instantly connect to anyone on the planet, but they need to be able to converse with others in their native language. We cannot ignore that they need to be communicatively competent. Knowing another language, or more than one, has never been more important. We must foster bilingualism by advocating for immersion language programs to be a mandatory part of curriculum, starting in early elementary grades or even pre-K, with a skilled language teacher. Colleges and universities must become more pro-active, in encouraging more education students to become language teachers. K-12 schools should encourage teachers to become skilled in other languages.

An essential book to read, that is a comprehensive account about the new kids and their role in the coming world, is *Children of the Fifth World: A Guide to the Coming Changes in Human Consciousness* by P. M. H. Atwater, L.H.D.

Parenting the New Kids: Why aren't my parenting skills working?

To call parenting new kids challenging is a glaring understatement. A parent of a new kid needs to be a therapist, an arbitrator, a mind reader, able to decipher behavior and translate conversations they do not understand and, oh yes, it helps to be a magician.

But, aren't these attributes that a typical parent needs anyway? Yes, but we would need to add that it would be helpful to be able to leap tall buildings in a single bound, in other words, a super human.

Since most of us aren't in that category, the best we can do if we can't stay a step ahead of them (almost impossible), is to at least be on the same wavelength. How do we do that? By educating and arming ourselves with as much information about how they think, what they need and how they want to be treated. We must try to understand, as well as possible, the world in which they live and what they need to navigate through it. An informed parent has a better chance to "survive" until they go off to college or work or another venue of their choice.

To be able to step into their realm, we need to look at the characteristics of these extraordinary individuals. Because of what they want to accomplish during their lifetimes, they do not see the point of spending their energy on practices that have repeatedly failed. They often see more effective ways to do things and rely on their intuition to get to the solutions, which is a direct conflict with the requirement in school to prove how they arrived at the answer. In fact, they do not see the need to have to prove anything and absolute authority is a problem for them.

If they are free to develop their true personality, new kids will utilize their boundless creativity and unique personal expression to begin to lay the foundation of their life's work. They need to be treated with respect. Even as very young children, they need to know that they are people of value and by listening to their opinions, we help satisfy their vital need to feel in control of their lives.

What will they *not* respond well to? It is clear that they reject inflexible rules, especially based on "that is the way it is supposed to be." Don't even try guilt trips, because they see right through them. Imposing your own agenda on them and any attempt to control them will only cause them to retreat. They simply will not attend to things they see no need for.

Because they are being forced to comply with such rigid standards, they are being side-tracked, even stopped, in trying to advance in their pursuit to fulfill their role as catalysts for change. This resulting frustration is behind many of these promising young people dropping out of school, experimenting with drugs and generally opting out. These are all signs of shutting down and seeking an alternate path for their lives, which many times sets up obstacles that can take many years or perhaps even a lifetime to overcome. What a waste of potential.

So, what *will* they respond positively to? They will always appreciate and react well to a constructive approach, explaining what you want them to do and enlist their help in completing the task. Being given options encourages them to participate in choices they make. Because they have a high level of frustration about the way things are, finding ways to help them to make a difference with something they care about helps to lessen their anxiety about the monumental task of changing the entire world. Encouraging or helping them to write letters to legislators to support laws that protect animals, for instance, or organizing a school focus group to address a concern, either in the school setting or in the community can be very empowering. *It is essential for them to feel that they are making a difference.*

One of the keys for interacting with the new kids is approaching them in a respectful and non-intrusive manner. Their propensity for extreme dislike of demands and authority speaks to their warrior spirit. They energetically engage in a meaningful activity or cause. They dedicate time and action to a goal and resist anything that deters them from reaching it.

Remember, they are here to shake up current social, economic and political structures and they innately know how they must proceed. They have very little patience for anyone forcing them to accept worn out methods and dogmas.

Up to now, it sounds like this parenting thing is all one sided. We cannot help to wonder how people so young can be so set in their ways. So do we not send them to school and let them be completely in charge, as they would like to be? As with everything in the universe, there must be balance.

Educators, scientists, doctors, parents and others who have observed these new kids for the past 30 years as students, in social situations and as members of a family, have offered opinions and options to assist them in achieving a sense of balance to their lives and to also help them adapt to the complicated world into which they were born.

A few suggestions to balance the power between the New Kids and parents:

- Even though they are very skilled, setting boundaries for themselves is very difficult. Bargaining for computer time at home, for instance, can help them to resolve other boundary issues. They are technological kids-born to use the computer, if left on their own, they will be on it day and night.

- Encourage them to interact with animals, art and nature. Because they can be loners, due to lack of "like-minded" young people in their lives, it can help to make a connection to another kind of reality, which may activate an interest in pursuing a hobby or even a career.

- Inspire them to keep a journal to share using different forms of writing including prose, poetry and memoirs as well as visual entries such as pictures from magazines, drawings, other art work or photographs. It validates that what they are writing or illustrating comes from their own perspective. It can be a great way for expressing their view of the world or to put into words or pictures what they cannot seem to verbalize. (A great activity for those who are very visual.)

- Help them control their extreme emotions, possibly through aromatherapy, meditation or quiet moments (see chapter nine), provide a low key environment in the home or a place they can retreat to when the family becomes too noisy. Encourage spending more time in sunlight, connecting to the Alpha brain state for stress reduction. (see chapter nine). Receiving or learning how to give Reiki can also reduce stress and promote a confident outlook (see: chapter thirteen).

- Make available physical activities that are good for brain-body coordination such as: dance, music, swimming, yoga, regular workouts, which we all need, but are very beneficial for the new kids to offset their high energy.

- Explain "why" about everything, they need reasons to engage, explain why certain rules of the house exist and enlist their input into possible changes, (good chance to negotiate), talk everything over with them, if they ask questions about rules that you feel you can't change, acknowledge their frustration. This also works when asked questions that you don't have an answer to. (remember, they are easily frustrated)

Basically, when all is said and done, what we are called upon to do is to love them and embrace their uniqueness and wonderful gifts and talents they possess. To accept who they are and help them to develop, without judgment, into the citizens of the Earth they need to be. To help them to settle into their extraordinary traits that will offer great changes to the world.

They also need help to come to grips with this new authority they bring with them, to avoid slowing down their progress by engaging in dysfunctional behavior. Most of all, we must be advocates for an education system that will encourage the fulfillment of their true intention, to help us all evolve to our higher purpose.

Dolores R. Card, Hermon R. Card

End of the Year

As I begin the annual archaeological
dig that is my end of the year clean up
I stare at the remnants
of the school year
trying to decide
the quality of the last ten months,
looking for clues
to tell me if what I had done
that had made a difference.

If I was smart
I would just dump everything paper
into the recycling bin
and all the rest
into the trash
and be done with it.

But I'm compelled
to examine everything
to determine its relevance
to my teaching.

Do I save it, recycle it, trash it?
(Isn't that the same question
I ask my students?)
It's tough to consign to the trash
the piece that she labored over
for three weeks,
grimacing
every time I called her to my desk
for a conference
until I finally half-smiled
at its almost-doneness
and told her "one more draft should do it."

Her sign of relief

The Missing Piece

scattered the papers on my desk
and her smile scattered my doubts.

Nothing to save from
the paltry output of one of my brightest students,
stuck in a self-defeating rut,
producing nothing but
heartache for mom,
frustration for me.
tears for himself.

I supposed I should have saved her poetry
for when she was able
to return for it,
but for now I just
read her cries of pain, her torment flowing
from line to line
like the tears on her anorexic cheeks.

How can his poem, a masterpiece only to him
filled with contrived
references to flatulence
be anything but trash?
Well, it is the best thing
he wrote.

So, for the twentieth or so time
I save everything—maybe not
in a box or folder,
but somewhere
within me, that place where teachers
keep everything that makes them a bit sad
to leave in June,
and a bit happy
to return in September.

The Poetry of Teaching
Herm Card, 1998

CHAPTER TWO

The Times, They Are A'Changin'
Bob Dylan

THE JOURNEY OF HUMANITY:
the New Kids through the ages.

Within every system and cycle on this planet, there is an expectation of evolution, which is a systematic growth of intelligence, skills and enlightenment. In each era of our history the Earth's energy moved in rhythm according to the needs essential for the advancement of our species.

Every civilization, through trial and error made discoveries to enhance their living conditions and ensure their survival. Walking upright was an early life-changing advance. According to fossil remains, the Australopithecus Afarensis may have been among the first. Remember Lucy, the 3.2 million-year-old-new kid from Ethiopia? (Imagine the looks of surprise on the faces of people on Main Street Ethiopia when the first person decided to stand upright to walk?) Along with the means of physical survival, the human species also gained insight into communication with others, once they discovered that there were other people on the planet with them. Gestures and guttural grunts were eventually replaced with a rudimentary language and my guess is a series of meaningful looks. The most important change was discovering love, the human emotion which is the enduring basis of life on this planet. Feeling and showing affection for another began to build a foundation for what we would eventually call relationships.

Scientific studies have shown that changes also took place in the human brain to meet the demands of each new phase of the era. Discoveries of human fossils have produced evidence that human brains, along with other anatomical changes, changed dramatically through the ages. It is called the process of encephalization. A rapid increase in brain sizes was noted in subsequent human fossils and at some point, it was noted, that the human brain had doubled its size.

Fast forward to the Middle Ages. The Earth needed inventive people to inspire a reawakening. Europe was deeply mired in the Dark Ages. Europe also needed a way to recover from the devastating black plague of the previous century. The quality of life was at a dangerous low. A cultural movement known as the Renaissance spanning from the 14th to the 17th century, began in Italy and then spread throughout Europe. The need for wider communication methods led to the invention of the printing press. Johannes Gutenberg, the new kid visionary from Germany, who loved to read, grew tired of waiting for another hand written volume, knew that there was a better and faster way to produce books. In 1450 he devised the printing press, probably the most significant invention of the century, which launched the beginnings of mass communication. It also fostered rapid development in science and art through the transmission of texts.

Literature, philosophy, art, music, science and other intellectual and creative pursuits were implemented by scholars and artists such as Michelangelo, Leonardo da Vinci and Petrarch, who were, by the way, also the new kids of the middle ages, bringing cultural changes and making way for a new method of learning known as humanism, which can be defined as a system of thought that centers on humans and their values, capacities and worth. Humanists emphasized the abilities of the human mind. Could the concept of modern education be far behind?

Other agents for change during the early years of the United States such as George Washington, Thomas Jefferson, Benjamin Franklin and so many others, all following their instincts about their role in shaping the time in which they lived.

In 1921 Albert Einstein (1879-1955) considered the most influential physicist, was awarded the Nobel Prize in physics. (It is always to my amusement to picture Einstein as a new kid) It brought the study of science to the attention of those interested in studying many different disciplines of science making way for students of the future to make choices for careers in science and related fields. This was especially true for female students.

As we advanced into more recent decades, even music evolved, as everything on Earth does, to match the energy wave of each decade and accelerate changes needed to be made. A musical agenda began to emerge and played an integral part in changing norms and sparking social and political upheaval. A look at the 20th century brings closer the changes that many of us witnessed or heard about first hand from parents or grandparents. We no longer had to rely on historians to make these events real.

The big bands of the '30s and '40s helped to soothe and reduce the stress of a nation enduring a major depression followed quickly by World War II. It was not until the mid 1930s that half of Americans were going to high school. We had a new and special class of people…teenagers. The radio became the friend of every teenager in the '50s and '60s. Their idols and icons were not perfect; they did not represent industrial moguls or CEOs of large companies or even upper middle class successful business men. However, needed changes did occur in spite of non-traditional heroes.

The appearance of Elvis on the scene in the mid '50s shook (sorry) that decade out of its repressive, staid, what-will-people-say mode. He was a new icon for the incoming new age. He changed the way we walked, talked and changed the beat of the country. He ushered in, through music, a global scale cultural transformation, which ignited new ways of thinking about who we were and how to get where we wanted to go. New, stronger feelings of unrest were building up to the '60s. The scene was set for a major social change.

Enter the tumultuous '60s. If ever in modern times there was a decade that was a crucial period, it was the 1960s. It widened the gap between parents and children that became known as the generation gap. The tool for transformation was music, written and performed by the new kids of the '60s. A shift was made from music being written by professional songwriters to self-written songs. We needed entrepreneurs that would affect the way that people thought and acted. We were not disappointed. Young people found their voice and American musicians like Bob Dylan, a most important agent of change of the times, filled that need, both through the poetic lyrics he wrote and his presence as representative of his generation. He became the spokesman for American youth and because he influenced the young, he affected the future. As his audience became older, many remained active in social issues as they matured into influential people themselves.

His song *The Times, They Are A'-Changin'* [1] became the anthem of the anti-war and civil rights movements. This song tells about universal truths that spans generations. It has relevance today as it did when it was written; it still fits perfectly to the current decade. This song is a plea and a warning—foreshadowing what we are now living through, the irony is that the times, in many important matters, have not changed.

His influence on '60s mores did not go unnoticed by "the establishment". He was nominated several times for the Nobel Peace Prize in literature and was awarded a Pulitzer Prize Special Citation for his profound effect on popular music and American culture.

Music was characteristic of the evolution that was happening. It was a time of rebellion and counter-culture in which young people were questioning everything. They were very aware that the status quo that had been in place for many decades was not working anymore and needed revision and, in some instances, elimination. Sound familiar?

In other countries their versions of the new kids were becoming apparent, especially in Great Britain. The recognition of unrest was becoming global. Interestingly, the most influential force on American music culture came through the British group, The Beatles. They were the new kids with Nehru jackets and mop top haircuts. They became an international phenomenon; no musical group can trace a more cultural effect right up to the present.

By the end of the '60s their music underwent a transformation as they grew and matured within their generation. They wrote songs about social inequities and rebellion against the political establishment. They became rooted in popular culture as their music became a symbol of the working and middle class way of life. Their music reflected the many emotions of people all over the world during a controversial and difficult era.

A major influence from another country was not surprising; it was the impetus to large-scale international connections, which would set in motion the increase in awareness that we are all inhabitants of the world and the need to work together for the greater good of us all. It represented a collective struggle by the younger people of the planet to speak for revisions of archaic systems that are counterproductive to the peace and well- being of humankind.

Those who taught the youth of the '60s, whose roots were at least a generation removed and were still immersed in the practice of mass education were puzzled why the "tried and true" education models they had been trained to use didn't seem to be as effective as in previous years. Many began to question their teaching skills and many left the profession discouraged and frustrated by this trend they didn't understand. Respect for the teaching profession began to decline, which was very unfortunate, as education methods sorely needed review and improvement.

The legacy of the '60s was its watchword: *freedom*, in all its forms. The new kids of that decade brought us from beginning to end through the storms and turmoil, some at great personal expense and sacrifice; for some, their very lives.

The new kids of the 1970s began the decade playing with an entirely new set of toys. The intensity of the anti-war energy pushed society in new directions. There was still, in Bob Dylan's words, *music in the cafes at night and revolution in the air*,[2] but as the war in Viet Nam wound down, it became a revolution in education.

The concepts of classical education were being questioned. Education professionals notably, Howard Gardner, were beginning to question the way people learn, and conversely, the way they should be educated. It was becoming clear that the traditional styles of educating people were not adequate for our increasingly non-traditional society.

Technology was the wave of the future and "Baby Boomers" like Steve Jobs, Bill Gates and Steve Wosniak, among others, were the catalysts for change. The personal computer would become the icon of the latter part of the 20th century and by the 21st century education took on a whole new energy and direction.

It is important to note that these significant new kids of their generation were educated in essentially nontraditional ways. Gates attended a prep school that allowed and encouraged students to indulge their expertise in the early days of computer science.

Jobs' early education consisted, to a great extent, of learning to tinker with electronics from his father, and learning to read from his mother. Ultimately a meeting with schoolmate Steve Wosniak, eventual inventor of the Apple computer, led to the creation of a technology that has totally changed the world of communication.

Larry Page and Sergey Brin, were both born in 1973, attended Montessori schools, and received much of their mathematical and scientific encouragement and inspiration from their parents. They tinkered, they invented, they experimented and they created Google, the massive search engine and the Internet media platform that has made information on every topic available to anyone able to connect to the Internet. It has been said, that in many ways, Google's effect on the world is of the same magnitude as Gutenberg's nearly 600 years ago.

Mark Zuckerberg, born in 1984, is said to be classically educated, hardly the norm today, combining scientific genius with a background in language and literature. Zuckerberg's experiments in programming computers in his Harvard dorm room led to Facebook, the social media platform that has helped create "the most connected generation in history".

It is certain that the 28-year-old Mark Zuckerberg in not the last new kid. Far from it. They are sitting in classrooms everywhere and their progression into becoming what they are intended to become is our responsibility. It is incumbent on educators—not just teachers but everyone who has a share in the responsibility to educate our youth, to accept that the agents for society's progression are among those we are currently educating. We are responsible for recognizing, accepting and encouraging them. If that requires that we change to accommodate them, then change we must.

There is nowhere to hide, all unethical practices will be revealed and rise to the surface to be appraised. We cannot improve what we are not aware of or cannot see, which is a main reason for the current chaotic condition of the world. Systems are being held up to the light to be revised, changed or eliminated. Our current education system is a primary example of one of those systems.

The charge of the new kids is to look at world systems and examine both their faults and their positive attributes and look into revisions, changes and even elimination of some that are no longer working; in other words, an overhaul of society.

The new kids will continue to increase in large numbers. Each generation will bring new inventions, medical breakthroughs and new viewpoints that have the promise of the elimination of fear-based patterns and the release of old belief systems.

We are Here to Stay.

There will no longer be only the small number of new kids in a generation, as needed in our past, to point out and make essential changes. Each person born into the human race from now on will be of the same succession until we no longer have the need to call them the new kids; as *they are us*. When we look at them, we are looking into the faces of who we are evolving into.

Transformational changes are needed in order to fulfill the vision of the coming world and it will take a concerted and long-term effort to affect these changes. This new world has great potential, but we will need people with foresight to make it happen. We must establish a clear purpose and sense of direction to build momentum for adjustments to many of our current patterns, attitudes and standards. Our current students are the torchbearers for this essential evolutionary progression. They come to this life fully equipped with all the resources required to live life to the fullest.

Would we not be remiss in our responsibility to advance the positive aspects of our society by hindering opportunities for the new kids to fulfill their potential and succeed in this effort? Amendment of our education system can provide those opportunities.

...and the world will live as one. Imagine, John Lennon[3]

Dolores R. Card, Hermon R. Card

The Graph Makers

He spends a great deal of time
wondering if he is
having any effect on them.

They are set up against
standards and tests
to measure them
relative to numbered scales
established by experts
who are convinced that
a graph will do just fine
for validating the success
or failure
of his teaching.

It might be better if the
graph makers
would just read Cassie's poem
about her dying friend
and have their hearts
skip a beat or two
at the opening line
and try to figure just where
on those x-y coordinates
to put that feeling.

...or else it's only a job.
Herm R. Card, 2006

CHAPTER THREE

To control and sort out young people for the sake of institutional efficiency is to crush the human spirit.
Ron Miller, educator

THE MISSING PIECE:
our spiritual nature; the nature of our spirituality

The meaning of spirituality is not about religion or religious beliefs. It is a much broader concept. Spirituality is what gives meaning to our life and leads us to go beyond our external identity. It touches that part of us that is not dependant on material things or physical comfort. It is when we feel completely at peace with who we are.

Expressions of spirituality can include meditation, prayer, religion and interactions with nature. It also includes pursuits that awaken our character and efforts to comfort, empower and inspire others.

Sharing a cup of coffee with a valued friend is a spiritual experience in that it satisfies our need to connect on a heart level; the heart being the symbol of the closest bond between human beings.

Spiritual matters are those that speak to our fundamental nature, free of ego, to be our true self. Spirituality kindles emotional responses that can include feelings of oneness, joy, acceptance and well being. Awakening our spiritual nature can help in dealing with difficult life challenges that come to all of us, such as a loss through a death or a major disappointment?

It is our spiritual nature that causes us to ask questions and express ideas about who we actually are and what is our role in the world. "What do I do while I am here?" We might ask about the deeper significance of life as we try to interpret our basic beliefs and gain insight into how we perceive the world around us. It helps us to move beyond our outward appearance and whatever façade we wear to fit into social norms.

Spirituality is a state of consciousness that sparks the need to know, to understand and most importantly, the need to be understood. Current education methods violate these very needs of students, as well as teachers; preventing them from bringing forth their spiritual dimension that would allow them to explore beyond the facts presented through present curricula.

Additional questions about our existence often include: how can I serve myself and the world, do I have the talent and skills to succeed, in other words, am I worthy? Students and teachers *are* asking these questions, and more, but they are asking them inwardly as there is no venue to address then in the outer world and, by no means, through the current education structure.

There is a prevailing fear that talking about the spiritual nature of the human being is somehow prohibited out of the context of some form of religious framework. Perhaps the reluctance of those in education administration lies in the fear of blurring the line that separates church and state. A concept we totally support.

However, what that suggests is that there is not a clear understanding of what spirituality means or the consequences of denying access, for both students and teachers, to that fundamental and essential part of every human being.

Evolution of Spirituality: spiritual awakening and enlightenment

Spiritual evolution is the theological idea that humankind evolved in consciousness along with physical, emotional and intellectual advancement.

When we are ready, we seek ways to awake to who and what we really are. Enlightenment helps to eliminate untruths and illusions. Many people are strengthening their ability to move past the familiar sense of the self, their families and their views of the world into a sense of reality and acceptance.

The experience of awakening differs from person to person. Every person is where they belong in their spiritual evolution. Therefore, no judgments or comparisons are needed. It is hard to describe to someone else when you begin to seek outside of yourself. The best description is that it is a shift in perspective, which is the heart of developing inner wisdom.

It sometimes takes a while to integrate new perspectives into everyday thinking. One must be willing to step into the unknown and be prepare to clash with your own beliefs and long-standing views about spiritual matters.

A true awakening can bring a sense of relief. It can stop the questioning; it's a done deal. A new perspective can bring other changes including noticing that things you previously loved to do no longer hold the same appeal. Not that they were wrong, but as your perspective changes, they may lose their importance. This also applies to relationships. We then tend to seek out like-minded people and activities where we can use more of our spiritual nature.

The key to permit awakening to happen is to attain a deep sense of relaxation by allowing everything to just *be*. The important thing to remember is that nothing has gone wrong; you are simply entering into the next phase of your journey.

Goethe, German writer, artist, politician and revered scientist in addressing the relationship of science to spirit wrote: *Science is as much an inner part of spiritual development as it is a discipline aimed at accumulating knowledge of the physical world.*

Add social studies, English, math, music, art and athletics and the same principle applies. Granted, Goethe was probably a new kid of his time, which is why he "gets it." Our education system also needs to "get it." How long would you continue to pay attention to someone telling you something irrelevant to your life?

I must confess that through the years as I attended countless seminars, lectures and conferences in my field, there were times when I opted to leave early. Usually, I would stay for lectures, out of respect for the presenters, as most were top-notch in their field, but many times I did not stay at or even attend workshops that I instinctively knew were not what I wanted to hear. They never got around to addressing how to help survivors utilize their spiritual nature to recover from personal violence. I must admit that sometimes, early in my career, I was one of those presenters, until I found my inner voice.

There is a voice we use to communicate through language. That is our physical voice. Yet, there is another voice that needs to be heard; our inner voice, one that speaks to us through our intuition and contains wisdom far beyond our physical capabilities.

Our inner voice never blurts out hurtful words, untruths or threats, while our physical voice frequently does not filter out what is being said. There is no need for a filter for our inner voice. It always speaks to our highest intention and always, without fail, the truth. It exists in silence for most people until it is coaxed and encouraged to express itself. Students need to find this voice.

If our students truly are "the most connected generation in history" as Eric Schmidt, CEO of Google, said in his 2012 commencement speech at Boston University, the connection must go beyond being able to "talk" to anyone around the world in seconds, but needs the kind of consecutiveness that includes the freedom to express the inner voice, which is not being said or heard much at the moment.

The Spiritual Lives of Teachers

Goethe: Teachers are our most valuable asset.

People become teachers through the heart. Teachers teach based on who they are within, no matter what the subject. There is no such thing as learning to bring spirituality into their classrooms. When they walk into any given classroom, they bring it with them, as part of themselves. It is not separate or something we learn to insert into our personhood, but we *can* learn to encourage and develop it. So often it lies dormant for years out of fear of reprisal or ridicule and we have to re-discover it and like muscles that haven't been used for a long time, exercise it and begin to bring it back to a state of healthy function.

Many of those who became teachers recognized in both themselves and their students that "missing piece" that was being ignored and suppressed, but felt helpless to introduce it into the system in which they worked. Newer teachers are part of the new kids' generation and are able to honor children on their life's path, as their energy is attuned to their students' energy. The dilemma is how to help those who set the standards for educating our children move beyond their comfort zone.

Some teachers have tried, through creating curricula that went deeper into the subject they were teaching, engaging students to explore the subject from their individual point of view. There is more to education than imparting information, there is a responsibility to use it as an opportunity to empower and provoke students to think with the heart as well as the mind. This kind of teaching takes teachers to a deeper level of their profession.

The Missing Piece

Young children are very connected to their spiritual selves. Many of us had extra-sensory experiences when we were young, but when we tried to bring it to someone's attention we were shushed or were told that we were weird or just imagining it. There was no choice but to shut down this mysterious, yet fascinating facet of ourselves. Children, even very young children, need to talk about such experiences without fear of reproach or judgment.

Tobin Hart P.HD., internationally known authority on spirituality, psychology and education wrote in his important book *The Secret Spiritual World of Children*:[1] *Children have spiritual capacities and experiences, profound moments that shape their lives in enduring ways.* I would add, those ways can be very positive or very negative, depending on how their experiences were received and supported.

Later in adult life, perhaps we are led to people, classes or books that validate our experiences and persuade us to begin to bring out that hidden but not forgotten part of ourselves. Such is the case with many teachers.

For a growing number of teachers, complying with these rigid standards and mandates has greatly damaged their passion for teaching and has left them frustrated and wondering if they have chosen the right profession. Discouraged teachers and students—what a formula for failure.

Training for new teachers needs to begin with the understanding that each person has chosen the teaching profession by an inner prompting that goes deeper than the old clichés about why people teach; such as "having their summers off".

Begin their training by exploring their own learning history, beliefs and theories about education. New teachers are part of the new kid generation; therefore, their basic instincts are the same. Their philosophies go hand in hand; they can develop and grow together.

Teachers reach into the next generation and beyond. They plant the seeds of thought and thinking. They have the ability to bring the world into the classroom to give students the opportunity to become more global in their perceptions.

They hold the future of this planet in their hands; we must free them to teach as it was meant to be. Students are non-traditional; so must teachers be allowed to be non-traditional in their approach to education. Some traditions are meant to be preserved and passed down, but when tradition becomes counter-productive to a society, there must be changes made.

If a child can't learn the way we teach, maybe we should teach the way they learn.
Ignacio "Nacho" Estrada

Please read about *The Respect Project: Envisioning a Teaching Profession for the 21st Century:* http://ed.gov/teaching/national-conversation

Defining the Margins

What is also clear is that there is a decline in social skills, manners and the setting of appropriate personal boundaries. Despite the facts that the new kids are highly intelligent, very intuitive, have amazing skills in science and math, many also lack the capability for amenable interactions with others.

They can be so attached to technology that the characteristics of their humanness are hidden beneath a façade of detachment, making it difficult to connect or bond with them. Because there are no boundaries for communicating instantly across the entire planet, personal boundaries are many times a difficult concept for them.

It's as if they are wearing blinders that do not allow them to realize what is happening on either side of them, keeping them focused only on to what is in their line of vision. The quandary is, do we just allow these new kids to do whatever they want and avoid education altogether? The answer is no.

How then do we nurture their spiritual nature and at the same time teach them to live in the society, tumultuous as it is, into which they were born? If they are to be able function well in this current social environment and still be able to fulfill their goals, there must be a balance.

Mentoring

New kids are inspired to pass along their knowledge as a means to make a difference. A good way to fulfill this need is through mentoring programs with younger students. Both younger and older students would benefit by being able to utilize some of their exceptional and perhaps their unconventional skills that they may have been suppressing.

While mentoring is an ancient archetype, originating in Greek Mythology, the practice of mentoring has changed considerably in the past 10 years. In addition to a formal type of mentoring for career success, aspects and reasons for mentoring have come to include effective relationships, sharing insight for learning and personal growth, which includes patterns for interactions with others.

The new kids' view of using drugs and engaging in sexual activity as "no big deal" is creating a framework for numbing their senses to what is important. The greater risk is that many are disconnecting from their emotional and nurturing aspects. While being detached is what may keep them focused on their tasks, it can also limit their awareness of their spiritual nature. They can become isolated and detached from reality.

The right kind of mentorship can help to close the gap between their drive to fix what they perceive is wrong and the means to live happy and contented lives. To mentor the new kids, it must be someone who can point the way by acting as a guide to influence and motivate and can serve as an example to demonstrate behavior, social skills, etc. It is not about their physical skills, but about attitudes and perceptions.

It must also be someone who is able to provoke a re-ordering of values by challenging them with new ideas to move beyond rigid ways of thinking. Mentoring cannot be used as a means to control or manage, it will not work.

Peer and group mentoring has been proven successful on all levels. Peer mentoring in high school must be provided by students who have been identified as being successful in social skills, interpersonal interactions and has proven to work well with younger students or in their own age group.

It is essential to remember that if peer mentoring is employed, *the mentors are, possibly, also new kids*. There are people in their generation who have, by whatever means, integrated appropriate values and behaviors into their character. Employing mentors for elementary students could be especially beneficial, as mentors could serve as positive role models before negative attitudes and behavior patterns are fully established.

An additional benefit of new kids mentoring new kids is their connection to like-minded people on a continual basis, which is a very crucial need. There would also be the possibility for long-lasting friendships to form. They could even become partners in learning in that each has the potential to be a role model for each other. Peer mentorship allows students to be freer to express ideas, ask questions and be more willing to take risks to see a different viewpoint than working with an adult mentor.

Mentoring programs with colleges can help to lower anxiety about making the transition from high school by becoming acquainted with the lifestyle and culture of college life.

There *must* also be an element of mentoring from parents and teachers. All children have promise, but they need stable and consistent adults in their lives to influence them in a positive and lasting way.

Adults can encourage and lead them to:

- learn listening skills
- open up new horizons beyond their social media devices
- understand the concept of family and appropriate behavior.
- acquire a sense of community

Children learn best by example, especially attitudes and conduct. Adults must model respect for others as well as self-respect. Self-respect has to be elevated to the highest importance. Self-esteem without the ego attached, but an inner knowing that one can be successful. Teachers and parents can be the demonstrators of these models.

Mentoring another person, regardless of the age of the person requires the understanding that in order to mentor, you must have had some degree of success in something. You are mentoring how success is achieved, the process of success; which may have little or nothing to do with academics.

The path to success is the same regardless of the area of discussion. If, for example, an athlete mentors a student who wants to become a good violinist, the traits of success are the same. Just as an athlete needs perseverance, commitment and motivation, so does a violinist.

Granted, mentoring requires a unique talent and commitment, but if we do not find people and ways to guide our current students, and their exceptional abilities, they may get lost in the upheaval and chaotic energy of our world. We have had the life experience to assess what is needed to make changes, but our students are new and are trying to become what their instincts tell them. Revising how they are educated and becoming their guides is the critical responsibility of our generation.

Enter Parents: they don't hand you a "how to" manual in the delivery room or with adoption documents

First, our children do not belong to us, they are not possessions, but rather complete individual beings that are in our care with the express responsibility to care for, love and nurture the promise for their lives.

Children are exposed to the worlds of violence, fame, sex and greed at an increasingly young age. It seems that childhood has shrunk down to a few precious years. They are bombarded by advertisements and other media and encouraged to behave stereotypically and look a certain way or they be deemed unacceptable to their peers. All of these things can and will shape their beliefs and behavior. By the way, they are bringing all of these images and beliefs to school with them.

Teaching and parenting are somewhat interchangeable—parents educate and teachers parent. The accountability of both is to nourish children's personal power. The Earth could be described as a big classroom where we are all perpetual students, including parents and teachers, hopefully preparing us to help others to awaken their inner nature.

As Thomas Merton, author, Franciscan monk and educator, who wrote extensively on the spirituality of education tells us *The purpose of education and parenting is to show a person how to define him/her self in relation to the world—not to impose a prefabricated definition of the world, still less, an arbitrary definition of the individual him/her self.* [2]

If we listen, the inner parent knows what is needed; the most important gift parents can give to a child is the freedom to find their way in the world. After we have fed them, kept them safe from harm, despite some of their questionable choices, and made the effort to provide a means for an education, our hope is that we have also instilled a sense of self-discipline so they may set needed boundaries as challenges come into their lives.

At some point, our work with their childhood is done and we look forward to establishing a different kind of relationship with our children, one of adult to adult. The truth? We never completely look at them as adults, they will, in some ways, always be 5 or 10 or 15 years old, depending on the situation that triggers that image. But, at the same time, we can still appreciate how they have conducted their lives and celebrate the wonder of watching them mature into the person they need to be.

Four years ago, my son-in-law, after dropping off his oldest daughter at college in Boston, said to me, through a voice filled with both sadness and pride, "Our lease is up. We had an 18 year lease and it is over, it is now up to her."

Children also have other "parents" as well as biological ones. They can be a neighbor who takes an interest in their lives, a coach or teacher who affirms their success or a friend or relative who recognizes a child's talents and encourages their interests. They all make an impression, some of them long lasting. Many people come in and out of our lives. Some stay for only a few moments and some for a lifetime, but each one has an effect on us in some way.

Parents and Schools

How many years have we entertained the concept of parents and teachers as partners? It is not only a good idea, it is essential to the progress of modern education.

Has it worked? Yes, up to a point. There are many factors to consider when assessing success of this model, geographic locations, environmental conditions, economic constraints, family beliefs and patterns are all reasons that can affect outcomes.

Schools make efforts to involve parents by inviting them to school functions, such as open houses, parent-teacher conferences, and after school activities. Other opportunities are school based organizations such as Parent Teacher Organizations (PTO).

These are all solid efforts to engage parents and promote a partnership. There are, however, glitches, such as parents not coming to parent/teacher meetings, parents who are overly critical of teachers and school districts and sadly, those who do not have the time or will not take the time to be involved with their children's efforts to become successful.

Another obstacle is that there is also a missing piece to parenting. Some parents are very aware about the spiritual nature of their children and that number is growing faster day by day. The problem is that these parents who are aware have no way to bring that awareness to the attention of their schools, teachers or administrators.

This creates a malfunctioning cycle. Parents who acknowledge and encourage their children's inner self, then send them to school where they are met with rigid rules and not much flexibility for developing critical thinking. That, at the least, stifles their child's creativity and sense of individuality.

This cycle does not constitute a partnership between parents and educators. They are not working from the same perspective or intention or perhaps from the same base of knowledge regarding the development of the whole child.

Parents need to practice the art of connection, of being in the present with a child, giving their full attention. They need to put down the magazine or turn off the TV, sit and talk to their child and actually look at them, without distractions. Making much needed alone time with each child builds their feeling of their importance in the family. Whenever a question arises from a child, the parent needs to stop whatever they are doing and turn their attention to the child. If it is not feasible to stop, they should explain why and choose a time, right then, to meet, talk and answer their question. The wise saying that "the greatest gift you can give to another person is your time," is essential in developing the parent/child relationship.

We are not naïve enough to believe that all parents have the skills to provide their children with these opportunities for personal growth. There are those who *become* parents without the background and skills needed to actually *be* parents. People are raising children without the awareness of the inner nature of both themselves and their children.

Whatever circumstances were present in the lives of those parents did not offer the opportunity to become aware of their own higher nature or to acquire the expertise to raise children. In many instances their childhood was, in large part, devoted to survival. Years of emotional and physical repression often result in a woundedness that interferes with and supersedes any efforts to understand the basics of the human condition.

The cost of this is the limitation that is placed on their children's lives, as well as their own. It is like trying to build a model without the directions. Some parents are learning subconsciously from their children, who are trying to follow their instincts and by example teach their parents, who may be struggling with their own sense of self-worth. Some of these parents were also children who were not accepted for their own spirituality and have closed down that part of their personality. Childhood should be a time of wonder and defining the world that is unfolding before them. For many, the effort to remain focused on the inner part of their character is obscured by trying to endure in their environment.

Unfortunately, the transformation of the human race does not occur all at once. Awareness of the self comes in increments, is not always discernible and is, at best, measured by sporadic moments of insight. Wouldn't it be wonderful if we become a world of enlightened people who knew instinctually what to do about everything at every given moment?

That day is on the way, but only after we have evolved to the point of changing old patterns and beliefs that have kept us mired in only our physical existence.

Sadly, there will be losses of some these bright minds that came to help through lack of willingness to understand them and provide them with the means and opportunities through a system that educates the whole person.

In the meantime, if we think of our generation as the pathfinders, the pioneers and, if you like, the new kids of *our* generation, who gives the current generation of students and teachers the blueprint to awaken spiritually as a species and begin the transition of our current civilization into one of mutual benefit.

Our education system is the key. *It is up to us.*

SECTION TWO

THE ART OF TEACHING

THE ACT OF TEACHING:
(Activities and Applications)

THE POETRY OF TEACHING

Dolores R. Card, Hermon R. Card

The Work of Teaching

Teaching is hard work,
demanding work,
unfinished work.

It is not work which fills me with
the acid-sharp eye-burning pulp mill air of Bogalusa
or the white-hot lung-searing auto plant air of Detroit
or the razor-cold blood-freezing ship yard air of Duluth

It doesn't lower me into the deadly dust and body breaking labor
of the coal mines of my great-great-grandfather in Wales
or his son in West Virginia.

I don't fear the limb devouring saw teeth
of my grandfather's mill
or the ulcerating tension of my father's law practice.

I do not share my wife's daily view
of the shattered lives of children.

I do not wallow in a miserable existence
born of hourly wages feeding too many mouths
nor labor in assembly-line tedium my intellect
collecting in a puddle at my feet.

I do not pray for the weekend's brief relief.
I pray instead,
for the strength to be patient
and the strength to be kind
and the strength to set an example

The Missing Piece

in a world where the example is often born of things that I DO fear—
ignorance and conceit
and prejudice and hatred
and abuse.

Teaching is not work born of fame.
There is no aspiration to glory,
no lavish movie star sidewalk recognition,
no numbers retired,
no laurels bestowed by Caesar.

Teaching is bearing the weight
of the world's children,
too heavy for most, but not for you and not for me.
Teaching is facing the demands of society
to cure its ills, to right its wrongs,
to solve what it cannot solve,
the hardest part, knowing
that the job never gets done.

Students do not roll out of the pulp mill in Bogalusa
or the auto plant in Detroit or the ship yard in Duluth.
Students roll out of my classroom
and your classroom.

They roll out of every classroom
in every city in the world,
and out of every classroom they roll
unfinished and incomplete,
because we are unable to put on
the final coat of paint
and buff them to the sheen
we would have them carry for life,
because they have built-in flaws,

Dolores R. Card, Hermon R. Card

and they have been imperfectly smelted and cured
and they are prone to rust and decay
and they have weaknesses below the surface
and they have been put together shoddily sometimes
and they have been whisked past the inspectors too rapidly
and given the final stamp of approval that simply means
they have been moved down the conveyor belt
to make room for more raw material.

In the acid-sharp, eye-burning air of Bogalusa
the pulp mill turns out a finished product.
In the white-hot, lung-searing air of Detroit
the auto plant turns out a finished product.
In the razor-cold, blood-freezing air of Duluth
the ship yard turns out a finished product.

But the product we turn out, flawed and imperfect
poorly refined, perhaps rough in texture,
is the most valuable product turned out anywhere

and it has a beauty and a texture and a gentleness
and a humanity that we give it even though
teaching is hard work,
demanding work,
unfinished work.

Herm Card
The Poetry of Teaching, 1998

CHAPTER FOUR

THE ART OF TEACHING

Much has been said about the outside forces that are causing much frustration among teachers and students. Anybody who has anything to do with the education of children knows what the problems are. We add our voices to those who honor the profession and to motivate our fellow teachers to believe in themselves and their students—to use the energy and inspiration within themselves to do what it is they love—to inspire students to learn.

There is nothing magic about it. It is and will continue to be hard work. There is no easy solution to the problems educators face, but there are means to accomplish our goals in spite of what might impede us—the ultimate solutions lie in the hands of those of us who have to face those problems every day.

Some Things to Think About

Philosophically, there is a Zen principle that is a key to effective education: *The journey is more important than the destination.*

The journey, the process of education, the experience, the day to day interaction of students and teachers, is where the learning takes place. How do we know if learning has taken place? The realistic answer is that we may not. We know when students have passed a test. We know how they have performed in class. We know if they achieve satisfactory scores on their assessment and other "high stakes" tests, but that doesn't mean they have *learned* anything.

The goal of education is to create people who can go out into the world and function within the context of that world. The ultimate assessment of our success as teachers will not take place for a long time after our students have left our classrooms. It will only take place as the generations of new kids have their effect on the world, the effect that we must enhance through our work as educators.

If we are to help our students on this journey, it is our obligation to make sure they are going in the right direction and at the end there is a fulfilling destination

The tricky part is that there is no single path that will get all of our students to the same destination. They must travel the road that is right for them, and we must guide their journey. We must understand that even though the destination may not be the same for all, it must be the best one for each.

Why Are We Here?

That is to say, why do we teach? Over the years I have asked hundreds of teachers that question. None have answered that they do it for the money or the fame or the vacations. None have answered that they do it for the piles of work to take home or the hours of their own time they put in, or the chance to spend their own money on supplies for their students.

They answer that they do it because they love kids, because they want to make a difference, because they are needed, because they were inspired by their own teachers. They answer that for all the right reasons they find themselves in front of students every day, doing their best to do the right thing to make their school better, their students better, themselves better—to make us all better.

The short version of my reason for becoming a teacher is that I had turned out to be too small to be a professional baseball player and my time in law school made it clear to me that the legal profession was not for me. I coached college baseball for a while and served in the military. I had skills in teaching that I had acquired in each of those professions, and genes inherited from three aunts who had been teachers.

At a friend's suggestion, I become a substitute teacher while I was looking for a job. A series of seemingly random, yet fortuitous events over the next several years enabled me to go from being a substitute to becoming a full time teacher. It became clear to me that I belonged in the classroom. I had not intended to become a teacher, and yet, I had. It was a classic case of being in the right place at the right time and I was fortunate to wind up in the profession I was supposed to be in, doing what I was supposed to do.

Today, such a career path would be very unusual. It is hardly likely that someone would stumble into a teaching career like I did. It is difficult enough to find a teaching job, let alone have the job find you.

To even enter the field in most states, prospective teachers are required to obtain a bachelors degree usually related to education, and satisfactorily undergo at least two pre-service teaching assignments (formerly "student teaching"). They are required to pass a difficult and diverse examination to receive their temporary certification.

To become permanently certified they must complete a masters degree in education and satisfy a number of stringent requirements, not the least of which is finding a teaching job, in which, they are evaluated as being worthy of permanent certification. Many complete their masters degree while teaching, which adds an entirely new dimension to their workload.

Then, finally, after their years of education, their degrees, their required examinations, their supervised experience, they begin to learn about teaching. There is no class that prepares them for the moment when they stand at the front of the room—their room—for the first time and the small voice in their head asks "Well, what am I going to do now?"

They look at the expectant faces—all eyes in the room trained on them. They are badly outnumbered, strangers in a strange land so to speak. The course in classroom management is now only a dim memory. The advice from mentor teachers is suddenly forgotten. The carefully prepared lesson plan is a blur on the page. Education theory becomes useless jargon. They are less than one minute into a thirty year career and they are stumped for an answer to that simplest of questions.

But what does not enter their mind is that they are in the wrong place at the wrong time—there is no place in their thinking for the words of the naysayers that students are failing, that teachers are failing, that education is failing, because at that moment—still in that first minute of that thirty-plus year career, they have the answer to that question—"What am I going to do now? I am going to teach."

And, fortunately for us, despite everything that seems conspiring to deter them, teach they do.

It Takes Courage to Teach.

Teaching requires conviction. It requires self confidence and a sense that one is doing the right thing in the right way for the right reasons. It requires the resolve to stand up to the fact that we live in a society that is all too ready to assign blame to teachers when the artificial standards that society sets are not met.

Even though we have somewhat devalued the term "hero," I am proud to wear a button that reads "Teachers are My Heroes." People are not heroes for doing the things they are expected to do—heroic acts go beyond the ordinary—they go beyond the day to day expectations—they embody the greater actions of selfless response to situations that are often beyond the ability of people to prepare for, or to comprehend.

It is intensely sad that it takes tragedy to enhance respect. It took the events of September 11, 2001 to make us accord first responders the respect they had long ago earned but had not received. Now it will have taken tragic events in Connecticut and Oklahoma to do the same for teachers.

Teachers have *always* been first responders. Other than parents, they are the first to respond to the critical need to educate our children, to guide them and lead them, to point them in the right direction.

In the Sandy Hook Elementary school, they were the first to respond to the violent armed assault on their school. It was an act beyond courage—it was the selfless response of people who care more about others then themselves. It was the response of people who, like parents, give no thought to personal safety when the safety of those they love is at risk. It was the response of people armed with nothing more than the need to protect helpless young people that led them to confront an armed maniac bare handed.

The true extent of their heroic actions will likely never be known. What is known is that they slowed the assault, impeded its progress, shielded and protected and comforted children and bought time for police to arrive. Six of them paid for that time with their lives, and others inevitably would have.

In the tragic tornado in Moore, Oklahoma, teachers reflexively used their own bodies to cover their students, shielding them from the deadly rubble crashing down upon them. They hadn't hired to be life savers, but there is something innate in teachers to protect those who need protecting. In Moore, their instinct was not to *seek* shelter, but to *be* shelter.

And so, we must understand that what was already a difficult job has now become more difficult because teaching will never again be the same. A sense of "what if" will infringe upon the day to day routine of education—the atmosphere, the energy, the very sense of what school is will change.

But—teachers will not change. They will continue to do what they do—what they love to do, what they must do. They will show up every day and focus their incredible energy on the young people in front of them—to educate and guide and lead.

And we will all pray that they will never again have to be heroes.

Crossing the "Rubric-Con": the fallacy of measurement

A few years back, I was consulting with the New York State Education Department and the company that produced the New York State ELA Assessment tests. A psychometrician from the company made a statement that the ELA tests were shifting the questions that measured writing ability from actual writing exercises to multiple choice questions. The rationale? The results of the objective-style multiple choice questions were much easier to graph than the subjective results of responses that had to be read and evaluated by teachers.

When I was serving as my school district's English department chairman, the assistant superintendent asked me to help him explain to the school board why our SAT scores were ten points lower that our neighboring, and rival, school district. He was concerned that for the last four years the scores had been approximately the same, and suddenly they had shot ahead of us. I told him the absolute truth—that I was the one responsible.

I explained that the district in question had hired me to teach an SAT preparation course. Half of their junior class had signed up for the course, and simply through understanding the strategy for taking the test, with no increase in knowledge, they had raised their scores an average of twenty points—an average of ten for the entire class.

He said he would find that difficult to explain to the board. I explained that the test was not a valid measurement of our students' (and especially our teachers') ability. Their students were no smarter than ours, just better prepared for the act of taking the test. Such is the fallacy of measurement.

Do better standardized test grades reflect better teaching or better preparing? Do class grades reflect better teaching or possibly subjective reaction to individual students?

When the concept of measuring students' success was originated, the stakes were not quite as high as they are today. The origin of grades in colleges was mostly to signify the level of qualification to move on to a chosen profession and grades were assigned by professors who worked closely with students and were totally familiar with their ability and achievement.

Similarly, K-12 teachers deal with individual students every day, and are sensitive to the entire process of the students' learning and aware of the difficulty and effort required to achieve success. Their ability to evaluate student performance based on appropriate means is an accepted and integral part of the education system, yet their assessments are considered insufficient when it comes time to evaluate a student's overall success in terms of meeting established standardized criteria.

As an example, suppose on a state's standardized physical education assessment test, jumping 4 feet on the test would be considered, "Highly Successful," 3 might be "Adequately Successful," 2 feet might be "Barely Successful," and less than that might be called "Lacking Success."

Also suppose that on the first day of the school year, Student X jumps 4 feet, and Student Y jumps 1 foot. It is clear that Student X is significantly better at jumping.

A few months later, taking the assessment test, Student X jumps 4 feet 2 inches and Student Y jumps 2 feet. According to the standards for the activity, Student X is considered *Highly Successful* and Student Y is considered only *Barely Successful*. What goes unrecognized and unrewarded is that Student X is rated at the highest level with miniscule improvement, while Student Y has improved by 100 percent and is considered to have barely succeeded

While Y has clearly accomplished more learning, the statistical analysis—the test's grading system, devalues the effort and achievement required to attain that *Barely Successful* level. The actual *degree* of learning is disregarded, as is the effort of both student and teacher to accomplish it.

So while the teacher apparently did a good job increasing Student Y's achievement, did that same teacher fail to do as good a job with Student X? Probably not. It was likely that student X was simply a better athlete than Y; more fit, bigger, stronger, more motivated and more skilled. Student X was clearly higher on the hierarchy of skills for that class than was Y, and it was the teacher's job to maintain and perhaps enhance the existing skill level as much as possible.

When it comes time to evaluate teachers, however, it's strictly a numbers game, and the better bit of teaching here will go unnoticed and unrewarded.

The Stakes of High Stakes Testing

High level education officials and test publishers may feel free to argue against this point, but the actual stakes of high stakes testing are entirely too high. Whatever evaluative benefit they claim is totally outweighed by the negative effect the "test season" has on students.

There are separate issues weighing on the situation—the issue of measuring students for their individual grade achievement, and the issue of measuring students for the sake of the state's assessment statistics.

The pressure to do well is generally not as negative an influence on students as is the excessive workload brought about by the pressure on teachers to "do well."

Thus, teachers are forced—"forced" being the operative word—to prepare students to succeed on their own grade level tests as well as to succeed on a state level test that has suddenly taken on major significance for teachers, though it has minimal importance for students. So—if you are a teacher—especially an early career teacher who needs to maximize your evaluation, what is more important—how students do on your grade level final or how they do on the "high stakes" state assessment that is part of your evaluation?

The catch, of course, is that the elementary and junior grade level test can determine whether they pass or fail your class (and maybe the entire grade), while the state assessment test has no effect on that. Of course, if too many fail your class, your evaluation won't be too good either.

For college bound high school students, the issue becomes even more serious. Grades are now an issue that may determine their college acceptance. The pressure to do well on high stakes tests becomes far more significant to them and their teachers. College acceptance rates make great graph material and key items on the "report card" states issue for individual schools.

So, in an attempt to maximize success at the time of year when students are already overworked, teachers assign more work, sending home practice tests along with regular homework, increasing an already too heavy workload.

Students are assigned entirely too much homework to begin with, but as test season rolls around, the additional assignment of review tests and other "practice" exercises, merely increases the load. Thus, the homework is no longer part of the learning process—it is part of the testing process, and learning—well that just is "validated" by remembering something long enough to enter it correctly on the test.

Time Peace?

In teaching, a time-honored profession,
for time immemorial,
there is no time, it has been said.
That's not true—there is plenty of time.
There is time for
room preparation,
faculty meetings,
professional sharing meetings,
parent conferences,
awards ceremonies,
"at risk" student meetings,
student council election speeches,
pre-observation conferences,
post-observation conferences,
10 fire drills and
other assorted evacuations,
review of the student handbook,
technology seminars,
schedule planning for next year,
superintendent's workshops,
the annual United Way pep talk
the annual "right to know" workshop
the annual campus emergency evacuation
occasional union meetings

individual student photos
group class photos,
photos for clubs,
and officers,
and sports,
and class notables,
(and who knows what else),
ELA prep,
ELA testing,
ELA scoring
ELA analysis
ditto for
state math assessments
state science assessments
state technology assessments
state social studies assessments
the class trip
the class picnic,
final exams,
room preparation,
faculty meetings,
professional sharing meetings,
and
maybe even some teaching.

...or else it's only a job.
Herm Card, 2006

Ouch!

It would be a rare teacher who has not had a phone call from parents explaining that clearly their child's grades are too low, and that admission to the school of their choice is essential for the child's future success and happiness. If you listen careful to student conversation, you will frequently hear an interesting pronoun/verb construction: *I got* an A in math. *He* or *she gave* me a C in math.

In my sophomore year in high school, my geometry teacher, "gave" me a 99 in geometry. I had 100s on every test, quiz and graded assignment except one. On that one quiz, I received a 99 because I had misspelled the word "isosceles." At the top of the paper were my grade and the comment "Ouch!"

After receiving my report card, I pleaded my case for changing my grade to 100, saying that since my average was 99.9 (to infinity) it should round off to 100. Logic seemed to be on my side.

In a matter-of-fact voice he said simply, "100 is perfect—and you weren't perfect." I profited more from his response than I ever would have if he had changed the grade.

While administrators and politicians like these things to be literal—charts and graphs are frequently their means of expression—the day-to-day success of teaching is far too subjective to be converted to specific number or letter grades.

We need to create a sense of accountability among students that is based on something other than numbers. They must become responsible for their actual learning, rather than suggesting that a test score is the defining acknowledgement of achievement.

In the army I was trained to drive a bulldozer. It is clear that the accountability here should have been my ability to actually perform the required tasks of a bulldozer operator. But, due to constraints on time and money, the final test was a 100 question multiple choice test. Does that sound familiar?

Ouch, for sure.

The National Pastime: where 30 percent is a pretty good grade

Baseball is a game that relies heavily on statistics to evaluate performance. Batting average (base hits divided by times at bat) is probably the most common means of determining success. Over time, the measurement formula has remained the same, but the factors affecting the batter's ability to succeed changed dramatically. In the '30s, games were played in daylight, pitchers tended to pitch entire games, travel was by train, fielder's gloves were small, games were played on grass, etc.

Eventually, night baseball was the norm, air travel took over, gloves got bigger, relief pitchers were specialists, the pitchers mound was lowered, performance enhancing drugs were introduced, baseballs were changed frequently, etc.

The means of performing—the relative ability of batters to succeed and, likewise, the ability of pitchers to prevent them from succeeding, changed drastically, but the measurement formula never changed.

Batting .300 (succeeding only 30 percent of the time) was considered the sign of excellence, even though the numbers of players able to do it declined steadily over the years. That is still the magic number, even though it is far more difficult to attain.

Evaluating education success is a similar misadventure in statistics, though substantially more inconsistent.

To measure academic success—let's use the term "knowledge" temporarily, a test must be administered—a test that is consistent across the board. This is simple enough in a classroom setting. A test is given, a grade is assigned. The students are evaluated against the standards established for that class in that school.

Once the need (or desire) arises to evaluate students on a large scale—state wide, for example, an entirely new and ungainly situation arises. To be fair, and accurate, it must be administered at the same time, under the same conditions. That means, for example, that the people who read the listening section, must do so under the same conditions, with equal fluency in English, with equal awareness as to the way to read it. They must do it consistently at every test site.

The people who grade the written parts of the test must be able to do so with common knowledge of what quality of writing is, with common background in the act of grading written pieces or in measuring the degree to which part credit might be awarded in math. (The reason for the graph maker's fondness for multiple choice responses)

None of this is possible. It simply can't be done. There is no way that all the factors of such tests can be equalized. So—the essential measuring tool is, at the beginning, invalid.

The fact that this measurement tool changes annually is also a factor that causes it to be invalid. It is impossible to create a test that is of exactly the same level of difficulty (or ease) from year to year. Thus, any attempt to measure the class of one year against the class of any other can't be done with the degree of accuracy claimed. It is neither logical not realistic to assume that can be done.

Teachers assume, subjectively, that a certain amount of learning has taken place when we see improvement, subjective improvement, over the course of the year. Students study, practice and they learn. It is extremely difficult to measure the *quality* of their thinking or the *quality* of their learning based on a test grade.

Naturally there must be a determination made as to whether or not a student has succeeded and should move on to the next grade. Since education is so thoroughly data driven, it's fairly important that sufficient numbers of students pass in order to make the quality of their education at least appear appropriate. I'm not suggesting that public education assessment is a form of shell game, but I am suggesting that the general public is far more accepting of objective factors than subjective ones, and far more likely to be affected by numbers on a graph than by the impassioned pleas of classroom teachers.

If data—numbers—is what we are basing our assessment of education on, how can we apply it to improvement in the classroom? The worth of the numbers generated by an inconsistent and invalid measuring tool might be summoned up this way. The key note speaker at a curriculum conference, a superintendent of schools for a rural district, put it like this: "I grew up on a farm. We didn't fatten our cows by weighing them."

The Results of State Assessment Tests Only Have Real Significance to Teachers, Administrators and Realtors.

Simply using test scores to evaluate the level of success of an activity is a useless reliance on quantitative rather than qualitative assessment—objective versus subjective.

So—the people who take on the responsibility for overseeing education devise means to measure the success in a literal sense, a sense that can be translated into charts and graphs and related to the general public in a form that reflects success compared to the standards that are set for such success

Over time, the tests have morphed into data instruments—the type of instrument where passing scores are determined ex post facto—a practice which allows for manipulation of levels of passing score to the point of absurdity.

The Missing Piece

Case in Point: a lesson plan for teaching irony

I was once part of a rather large group of teachers that met in the state capital to perform the act of standard setting. That means that we went through a rather laborious process over several days, to actually take the tests, and make judgments as to the difficulty of each question, and determine the likely percent of success by typical students on each one. We discussed, dissected and analyzed each one, and ultimately, decided on a numeric relationship between each of the four measurement levels on the test. Then we determined the "passing" grades for the test.

When we had accomplished this and reported it, the education official in charge said that since the scores had improved significantly over past years that he felt it might be hard to "sell" the scores to the public. The irony was overwhelming.

We questioned this incredible statement by suggesting that since over the previous 5 years teachers had been working with the State Education Department's new guidelines to accomplished just such an outcome, they should be proud to release the results since this was their goal. He responded, somewhat vaguely, that it was the public skepticism—the public who clamored for improvement—that would make it difficult to accept dramatic improvement

Two weeks later, when the scores were released, they had been lowered. The success that teachers and students had apparently achieved was negated by the fact that since the public responds to numbers, only numbers than can accept can be used. The apparent success was negated by the fear by officials that the people who wanted improvement would not believe it.

Reality, actual reality, is performance based, and as a society, we like the clarity of a good graph over the need to actually understand a narrative evaluation.

Thus, the system itself calls into question its own validity. If individuals can determine results, they can also determine what to do with the results, how to slant the results and what the ultimate outcome of the results can be.

Don't Confuse Standards with Curriculum

Standards are goals—somewhat measurable mileposts in education that have nothing to do with what is actually taught or how it is taught. Setting standards should not establish curriculum.

Once administrators get into the mix, they tend to misinterpret the idea of standards and begin to misunderstand their role in the process. Administrators (other than those specifically tasked as such) are not necessarily curriculum experts. They may be able to monitor curricula, but they should not be autonomous curriculum setters or teaching evaluators. Much like corporate CEOs, they are responsible for profitability without necessarily understanding what's happening on the assembly line.

Education in the Long Run

The Latin origin of our present day "curriculum" is the word *currere*, meaning "to run," as in running a race. Our own version of "run" can also refer to the act of operating or managing something. Thus, the juxtaposition of ancient and modern meanings leave us with the ironic sense that people who run schools do so with an eye to managing the curricula of those schools. They try to create a set of courses and subjects that include everything important for students to learn. They like the nice progression from year to year that can be evaluated every June, and those graphs can be created and published for the coming year.

When learning standards were first introduced in New York State, there were some 75 distinct items that could be taught in eighth grade ELA. They could be itemized and checked off as they were covered, thus insuring that significant teaching had taken place. Good teaching cannot be done that way—teaching a unit, testing the material, checking it off the list and moving on.

The performance of many teachers is inhibited by the insistence that they adhere to a test oriented curriculum. A test oriented curriculum tends to defy the logic of a student oriented, performance based curriculum and prevents teachers from being involved in the learning process in a way that truly reflects their own engagement.

Climbing to the Top

Over the period of students' school careers, the curriculum is designed to enable them to progress upward through the subject hierarchy. In order for students to progress, they must be given a means to do so.

Think of schooling as a series of stairways leading up from one floor to the next—negotiating each stairway indicates improvement, and arriving at a new floor shows a new level of achievement. But consider also that climbing those stairs can be a challenge—not everyone is equally capable of accomplishing the climb at the same rate or with the same ease of effort.

Anyone who has ever climbed to the top of the Washington Monument or the dome of St Paul's in London understands the difference between easy and difficult. Stairways can be just plain old stairways, easy and short, while others are long, winding, narrow, steep.

Each school "stairway" has unique challenges. Everyone deserves the opportunity to reach the top and there must be assistance for those who are unable to climb as easily as others. Teachers provide the assistance, but students must make the climb. If it is too easy, there is nothing gained. We offer them the means and the opportunity to prove to themselves that they are able to make the climb.

An effective curriculum must have horizontal components as well as the vertical, year to year aspect—one piece laying the groundwork and support for others down the line. For example if we teach poetry as a distinct, standalone unit, we deprive students of the opportunity to discover the poetic language in all literature—how can we dismiss the poetic language of *Moby Dick* or *To Kill A Mockingbird* or *The Red Badge of Courage* as simply prose?

The vertical curriculum builds on itself from year to year. Learning the alphabet in pre-k leads to spelling and reading in kindergarten and other lower grades. Learning addition and subtraction skills will eventually lead to performing high level calculus computations. As the years progress, the vertical aspect of the curriculum leads to reading more diverse and difficult works from grade to grade.

Oversimplifying what we teach does a disservice to students. The essence of a productive curriculum is that it offers substantive content and a means to allow the students to absorb the content in a way that validates the experience. Learning for the sake of learning is a weak concept.

Considering the vast reservoir of possible "learnable" content in a curriculum, the task of deciding what to teach is not only intimidating, it is mind boggling. Sorting out specific content to teach becomes a nearly impossible task. Creating curriculum standards and learning standards likewise becomes a monumental task. Who is qualified to do that?

Creating a universal curriculum to achieve universal results ignores the concept of individual learning styles and individual needs. Only by implementing education that is pertinent on a local level, will we develop education that is successful on a global level.

Those That Can, Teach

Baseball Hall of Famer Honus Wagner said "There ain't nothing to being a ballplayer—if you're a ballplayer."

The same thinking can be applied to teaching. For the most part, we are teachers because we are supposed to be teachers. We have the skills, the desire, the energy, the knowledge, the presence and all the other things needed for our profession.

It is not an easy thing to stand in front of a classroom for the first time. It is not necessarily ever completely easy. What it does get, is easier, and it gets that way through experience. Practice, the sheer act of correctly repeating an activity, makes one better at it and with that improvement comes confidence. Athletes, musicians, chefs—most skilled practitioners—learn through repetition. But, it must be repetition of successful actions. Simply doing something over and over again does not make it successful, it simply makes it consistent.

People become highly skilled by repeating successful actions. In order to repeat successful actions, we must somehow understand that an action is successful, and we must also understand why it is successful. This is part of the innate sense of "being" a teacher

Teachers must have the insight to understand that failure—academic failure—is built in to the process. We must be willing to accept that and not let it undermine our sense of self worth. We must have the spiritual courage to accept that we are not infallible—students will not learn simply because we want them to—force of will is not always the deciding factor.

Self assessment is essential, but not necessarily easy. We are all aware of how we *should* be teaching, but, unfortunately, that is not always the easiest thing, particularly when teachers themselves are being evaluated based on somewhat artificial means.

Since all teaching cannot take place on a single plane, we must, depending on the curriculum, deal with specific needs and talents at specific grade levels.

Years ago, when daily journal writing was introduced as a stimulus to creative thought, it became incredibly popular and eventually, overused. It frequently became an exercise in cursory fulfillment of assigned tasks on topics to which students could not adequately relate. They were not able to think diversely enough to gain any benefit from the assignments. They focused literally on the topic, and wrote, whether or not they had much to say.

Rather than being a springboard to creative thinking, it became something of an impediment. Anything one does every day, in the same fashion, will become decreasingly exciting and decreasingly inspiring. There is much to be said for dogged determination, but school is not always the place for it. Students are far more likely to just plug away to nowhere. They are usually not confident questioners, so they are far less likely to ask "Why?" than they are to ask, "How long does it have to be?" and then make it the way they think the teacher wants it to be

Good teaching and effective learning require a sense of what *does* work as opposed to what *is* work. As we develop a better sense for that we become better teachers. What works is anything that inspires the students to engage in the learning process in a productive manner—productive qualitatively rather than quantitatively. Thus, they become part of the process, learning from within themselves rather than from simply within the topic.

What *is* work is an assignment to which the student cannot relate or has no knowledge related to it. Even a research paper topic should be based on something relevant to the student, not something that is designed to simply compel him or her to seek out facts and arrange them on paper. Likewise, the idea that we must assign homework because it is traditional creates work for students and teachers alike, but does not necessarily produce effective results,

In order to successfully enhance quality and decrease ineffective quantity, there must be freedom of thought and freedom of choice. The most successful learning activities are those that allow the students to engage themselves in inspired thinking. By allowing them to let their minds, and their resulting ideas, wander where they need to go, they become far more willing to explore. Their learning will be driven by their own energy and the result will truly be their best work.

Poets Were the First Teachers of Mankind

When the ancient Roman poet Horace (Quintus Horatius Flaccus) said that *Poets were the first teachers of mankind*, he was delivering words that would be an appropriate mantra for today. While the dictionary defines poets as people who *write* poetry, it is more appropriate to consider poets as people who *sense* poetry. In the same way, teachers and students are far more successful when we have a sense for learning rather than just going through the act of learning.

We tend to define school subjects in terms of our own perceptions. For example, we tend to label English as creative and free thinking and math as literal and structured. There is, of course, some truth to that. There is a difference between the ideas that *a rose is a rose is a rose* and *two plus two is four*. Gertrude Stein created an image and some ancient mathematician created a rule.

There is much room for creative thought in the way we consider a rose. There is no creativity to the addition rule, but it is likely that both the rose metaphor and the math rule could create questions in students' minds. "Why" is a likely one. School should allow us to be creative, especially the new kids who are a poetic generation and we should be encouraged to share that creativity.

There is definitely a literal side to school, at least to its process. Educators need to provide the freedom of creativity. We need to allow students to ask about the rose metaphor and the math rule with equal ability.

Given the opportunity to be creative, one is also given the opportunity to "go public" with the work. While the standards recognize the need, and require the public interaction of one's creative work, the standards do not address the method for which these activities are comfortably undertaken.

To simply make statement that students *will* do something does not address the *how* or *under what conditions* part that is a critical aspect of every activity. As teachers, we must insure that students can exist in a comfortable environment. Here is where the poetic nature comes in. What do we consider *poetic* to be?

Whatever your definition might be, it is unlikely that such words as *discipline, strict, orderly* or *attentive*. These are management words, with no sense to them of poetic nature. They are, of course, necessary for a class to function, but by themselves do not foster an environment in which it is comfortable for the students to achieve.

We have to understand that legitimate learning relies on a bit of risk taking by the students. For students to stand up for their ideas, defend the credibility of statements, verify sources, et cetera, they must put themselves in a position, which exposes them to the possibility of being wrong. For students to speak in public, to read in public, to discuss issues in public exposes them to the possibility of being publicly wrong. In a group of people who are intensely conscious of the need to be *right*, the prospect of being wrong is quite intimidating.

A few years ago a former student of mine came to me for some advice as to which of two pieces of writing she should submit to the *Scholastic* writing contest. I read both carefully, considered the voice, the choice of audience, the tone—everything a judge would consider. I told her which of the two I preferred.

It was a spectacularly well-written piece analyzing the relationships of the educational system to students, by comparing a teacher and a student to an elephant keeper and a captive elephant. It was compelling and ironic, with a voice far beyond that of the typical ninth grader. It compared the thoughts of the teacher and the student about each other to the thoughts of the keeper and the elephant. The other piece was a dryly-humorous piece about music lessons that I found difficult to understand and advised against it as her entry. You should be able to figure this out by now. The piece I did not recommend, or even particularly like, won one of the gold awards given to ten of the some 20,000 entries.

However, some twenty years later, her other piece has shown her ironic prescience.

The elephant died because the keeper was so certain that he was doing the right thing for the elephant that he neglected to provide what the elephant really needed. He cared more about being right than he did about doing right. I liked it because it spoke of something I knew about and believed in. She chose the one that was more about something she knew about and believed in.

Clearly, my own preferences and lack of understanding of her piece skewed my ability to allow her to make the decision that she was ultimately able to make on her own. She knew what was best for her and didn't let my advice lead her astray. She displayed the "new kid" courage that allowed her to move forward. She was typically underserved by her school, but persevered, knowing that she was right. She is now a college professor.

The ironic thing about student work and judging that which is best is that "best" is such an incredibly subjective term.

Therefore, assignments, which generate the "best" work, are likewise subjective, depending upon the goals, perspective and philosophy of the individual teacher, but ultimately hinging on the goals, perspective, philosophy and ability of the individual student.

The "best" student writing, in my classroom, was writing that while, of course, using the correct standards of written English also spoke the words of the student as they flowed from the students heart and soul, rather than from the students brain. I know there is a slightly trite dreaminess about that statement, but I firmly believe that if students are allowed, and encouraged to respond from within, they will produce their best work.

Certainly there are mechanically talented students whose every piece of work will be of the highest quality I was inclined to not enjoy the act, and art, of teaching, I might want a classroom full of such students, because I probably would not have much to do.

I have received praise for the work I have done with such students, and honesty usually compels me to say that the best thing I did for that student was to get out of his or her way and allow them to use the talent that they had already brought to the work.

We Should Encourage Students To:

Trust in the process.
The Zen philosophy is that we learn through the journey, not at the destination. Learning takes place in the process, not in the assessment. The student who cannot relate to the task will be discouraged easily, and will not willingly enter into the learning process. By providing the student an opportunity to connect to the desired learning, we also provide him/her with the opportunity and incentive to succeed.

Make connections to themselves
Introspection leads to individual reality, rather than the mass reality that is expected of students by assessment tests. By encouraging students to engage in introspective thinking and providing learning activities that connect them to the world around them, they are better able to achieve learning that is realistic in the finest sense, and becomes *relative*, rather than *reflexive*.

Work beyond themselves to extend their reach
By creating expectations that seem (to them) somewhat beyond them, and allow them the opportunity to *safely* falter on the way to achieving these goals, we strengthen them as learners. If we become their coaches we are on the right track. If we become their editors we are not, because the job of the editor is to ultimately create a finished product, and too frequently, that becomes *our* product.

Work with us, not for us
Self esteem can become over-rated if students are simply told that they are "good." Students do not become "good" by being told they are. We must offer them the means and the opportunity to prove to themselves that they are good. If we share the fact that even teachers have struggled with certain parts of their education, students become more willing to take chances and less afraid of being "wrong." They will be less likely to view themselves as less skilled if we assure them that they are merely less experienced. This empowerment gives students the freedom and ability to use their own resources to be successful, and to trust in themselves as they come to trust in us.

We Should Encourage Ourselves To:

Not confuse different with difficult

The tendency to stereotype "different" students is risky—these are more than likely to be the students that will challenge you to be better, rather than challenge you in the traditional sense of being difficult to deal with.

"Difficult" is a relative term—what may be difficult to some will be easy to others. No one experiences learning on the same level. One of the true challenges to good teaching is the need to approach each lesson with the knowledge that one must predict what might create difficulty for the students. Difficulty may be the very thing that leads to improvement by you and your students. Think of the practice sessions people employ in any number of endeavors. At first nearly anything we try that is not instinctive is difficult to a degree.

Think of the things you do—skiing, playing the piano, rock climbing, knitting, teaching. Were they "easy" when you first tried them? Not likely. Did they become easier with practice?

Difficulty is the challenge. If students are difficult to teach because their skills are advanced, so much the better. Those differences should serve to enhance education, not obstruct it. Recognizing the "difference" is one thing—accepting it is another. Being open to accepting their difference is the key to teaching the new kids. One of the most important things to remember about dealing with new kids is that they may only be "new" to you.

Accept challenge as opportunity:

We improve by being challenged and overcoming that challenge. We get better by being pushed to get better. Committed teachers need to recognize that new kids challenge them in a positive way, not in a threatening way.

Teachers are not always comfortable with the idea that answers can just pop into somebody's head. There is a concern for their responsibility to have done the teaching—that somehow if the student came up with an answer without being "taught," something is amiss. It is important to understand that someone arriving in class with a high degree of innate talent should not pose a threat, but rather an opportunity.

It can be somewhat discouraging to realize that there is untapped potential in a student that we are not serving, and it should be. The challenge to work "up" to the level of students is the very challenge that will ultimately enable us to teach ALL our students better.

Be realistic:

Enabling and encouraging students to think requires providing with a reason for them to do so. The idea that education stands alone is no longer valid.

Learning "because you need to know it" should justifiably be followed by the question "why do I need to know it?" "Because it will be on the test," is another poor response especially if the reference is to state level assessment testing which has no relevance to most students.

Students seek success that can only come through achievement of certain goals, and the setting of those goals should take into consideration the needs of the students. Determining those needs is crucial in determining what the curriculum should be, and what the appropriate measurement standard should be. Ideally, curriculum must be tailored to the student, but it also should to be tailored to the community.

Means for Students to Succeed Against an Essentially Unfair System of Measurement (students are not data)

It is imperative that we provide students the opportunity to succeed. In order to do that we need to allow them to participate in class safely. Students tend to be afraid to share because they are afraid of being wrong—and the ensuing negative feedback from tracers' and peers.

As much as possible students should be allowed to begin assignments during class time. That reduces the chance that they will be unsure of the assignment or what is expected of them. It eliminates the frustration of not understanding and being unable to complete it as homework. It also enables the teacher to confirm that they have begun the assignment—and reduces the opportunity for students to say that they didn't understand as an excuse for not completing the assignment.

On in-class work, the teacher should "scout out" correct response on the students' papers and ask for responses from among those students. This also enables the teacher to engage reluctant responders to participate, since they can assume their answer will be a good one. It is also possible to "ask" students to participate while going around the room, affirming for them in advance that their participation will be successful.

A good means for comfortably sharing student work is to have the students write their responses on transparencies or other media that can take advantage of an ELMO, if available. They can read their work from the back of the room while the other students read their words on the screen

Thus, the students are not intimidated by being in front of the class, and the class is able to read the piece which overcomes the difficulty some students might have in reading the piece even from the back of the room.

Removing threats encourages participation—assuring successful participation engendered trust and encourages future participation.

It is important that students understand that they are working with us, not for us. There is a common goal—that goal is to be successful as a student. The less emphasis placed on test preparation—the less emphasis placed on stated test success, and certainly the less emphasis placed on the fact that teacher evaluation is tied to student success.

Student success, in a realistic sense, cannot be accurately measured. The ultimate measure of student success can only be seen in the way they ultimately function in society. An upturn in the sense of society reflects success in education. But—how is this measurable? It really isn't. So—the people who take on the responsibility for overseeing education devise means to measure the success in a literal sense, a sense that can be translated into charts and graphs and reported to the general public in a form that reflects success compared to the standards that are set for such success.

Think

In the 1950s, on the wall of practically every school room in the Triples Cities of New York (Endicott, Johnson City and Binghamton) was a simple white sign with black capital letters that read "THINK." That was the motto of International Business Machines (IBM) the global computer giant that, like me, grew up in the Southern Tier of New York.

The motto is simple and logical, and it became the mantra of a developing computer giant. It is also a key to the development and success of an educational system.

The essential element of education is providing the stimulus to students to do that very thing—to think—to engage in the logical progression of ideas from the posing of a problem to its eventual solution.

As with most physical skills, thinking cannot be actually taught any more than someone can be taught to be agile. However, like any physical skill, it can be enhanced in the classroom, through coaching and experience. Educators try to enable students to think in logical and productive ways. Simply telling someone to think, in order to get an answer, is only effective if the meaning of "think" is clear to them—and if they are comfortable in actually doing it.

The "THINK" sign on my classroom wall was paired with a sign, updated every year, that read: *We have not had a thinking related injury in (X number) years.* Sometimes it required students to actually think a bit to figure out what the implication of the sign was, but that in itself was a step in the right direction.

Encouraging students to think, as distinguished from daydreaming, generally only works if there is a reason to think. They should recognize the likelihood of a successful and meaningful outcome to the thinking. Not everyone is Sherlock Holmes, though. People can only think according to their innate ability to do so, but they *can* develop better reasoning skills, skills that allow them to "THINK" to the maximum effect. They just need to be provided a means for maximizing their skills.

Teachers need to model the process that they use in a way that allows the student to follow their reasoning sequence. As a college freshman, I was overwhelmed in my required basic psychology class, because I was not adequately equipped to follow the intricate instructions of a trained and experienced logician. He neither modeled nor taught the skills required, assuming that since we were in a college class we were adequately equipped to learn what had taken him years of study to perfect. We teachers cannot assume that students are equipped to learn through a singular method just because it worked for us.

Remember—what we teachers do now as a matter of reflex was once new to us. We learned it as a step by step process that we refined through practice and experience. Thus, even though when we started we were prepared to teach, we were not necessarily prepared, or able, to teach well.

Just as our students do, we started out unskilled and worked our way up the skill hierarchy through experience. Just as we were motivated to progress, to get better, we need to show them a reason to progress, a reason that relate to them in a way that makes sense. We must provide them a reason to engage in learning, and a safe way to fail on occasion, without discouraging them from continuing.

I was once told by a "test person" from a test-writing firm that *reading comprehension test questions should not be worded so that students can figure out the answers.*

This is clearly the thinking of a statistician, rather than an educator. It goes against what we try to instill in our students. The concept that a student should not be able to answer questions by figuring out the answer is inane, at best.

Our goal as educators is to enable them to do just that, and the faster the better. Being able to do it without consciously thinking about what they are doing is the ultimate goal. For some, the solution just pops into their heads, while others must research or think through the process to solving it. There are few situations in life that grant "part credit" for showing your work, as on a math test. If someone is required to solve a problem at work, it is essentially unimportant (within bounds of proper ethical conduct, of course) how they do it.

We Live in an Information Age, But What Determines if We Live in a Learning Age?

Because we live in what has called the "most connected generation in history," access to information is practically instantaneous. Students are able to answer questions with the click of a button. The corporate name of the largest search engine in the world has become a verb, but *I Googled it* is not an acceptable response to validate learning.

Even though acquiring information is part of the problem solving process, the key to learning is the retention of the information. Access to information should never be confused with knowledge. Getting the answer to a question from the Internet guarantees neither the validity of the answer nor the understanding by the student.

If a student is merely the conduit for passing information from a computer to the paper, or to the teacher or whomever, how much of the information actually sticks where it should, with the student? Learning only takes place when information is retained—the goal of assessment testing is to measure that retention, but what legitimizes the testing? True learning only takes place when the information can be utilized in a means that demonstrates that it has been retained and can be applied to situations that make it useful. Otherwise it is just retention.

Most Assessment Testing Methods Require Retention but Not Necessarily Learning.

Telling a class that they will need certain information to do well on an upcoming test merely gives them the idea that they need to retain it to succeed on the test itself, not that they need to learn it for any purpose beyond the day of the test.

I had taught ten years in high school when (as department chair) I decided to transfer myself back to my teaching "roots"—eighth grade. As part of the move, I adjusted the curriculum to allow me to also transfer Ray Bradbury's *Fahrenheit-451* to the eight grade curriculum. For the first (of several) time in my career, some teachers advised me that I shouldn't do that because the book was too difficult for eighth graders. Some even suggested that it had been too difficult for 9th and 10th graders.

Here's where I question the system—who says it, or anything, is too difficult? Fortunately, as department chair, the decision was mine. I took it as a challenge of sorts, but knew that the book was not only "teachable" but it was important that students read of it and be aware of its message.

The teaching part was a matter of making the students aware of what the book was "about" and allowing them to follow the trail that related to their own lives. By allowing them to realize for themselves that they were surrounded by the very technology and consequences of it that Bradbury had predicted in the early 1950s, they were able to understand it far better than if I had simply taught it to them.

The process of discovery is essential to education. For students to realize that they have learned something, rather than having had it taught to them is invaluable. It is also encouraging to them to understand that they have the capability to in some ways, manage their own education. The relevance of the subject matter—the "What's in it for me?" part, allows students to pursue the goal far more willingly.

Students need relevant connections to their learning. They are frequently more discerning in their approach to learning than we give them credit for. That is part of the challenge for educators—to understand better what *needs* to be taught, rather than what *has* to be taught.

I find it astonishing that people are able to make those decisions about curriculum. Who is it that decides? How do they decide what needs to be taught and how it has to be taught? There is so much history, for example, and more every day. What are the best novels, the best poems? What are the most important science experiments? What math is most useful? What exercises are the most energizing? What diets are the healthiest?

Unfortunately, it tends to be the people that control the money—the political end of the spectrum. The people who are appointed to these jobs are directly connected to people who have been elected to govern—those who we have elected to supervise our society also get to supervise our schools and the education provided therein. Expertise in government management does not necessarily indicate expertise in education management.

We Must be Activists for the Right Curriculum:

Students seek success—success can only come through achievement of certain goals, but the setting of those goals needs to take into consideration the needs of the students. Determining those needs is crucial in determining what the curriculum should be, and what the appropriate measurement standard should be. Ideally, curriculum needs to be tailored to the student, but it also needs to be tailored to the community.

Urban schools require urban oriented curriculum—suburban schools and rural schools must likewise be considered on the basis of student needs and student demographics rather than an all-encompassing standard.

All educators need to take a more assertive stance to make sure our students learn what they need to learn.

It Could Have Ended Better

On the last day I was in my former school as a full time teacher, I wanted to wish the three new English teachers well—to congratulate them on the beginning of what I hoped would be long, energetic, satisfying careers. I wanted to share a moment with them that might assure me that what had been so important to me was going to be in good hands. I intended to remind them that even though they would face test pressure and assessment pressure and standards pressure, they would have the have the ability to face it and win, because they were young and energetic and talented and able to invest all of that in their students.

I found them surrounded by the huge pile of new textbooks and the large boxes of prepared curricula that the principal had ordered for them. There was a box for each that contained lesson plans, transparencies, literature work sheets, guides of all types that would enable them to teach the skills that whatever company had provided the materials determined were in line with the state's ELA standards.

Assuming that they adhered to the guidelines that the principal apparently felt were worth the significant cash outlay for the materials, they would be able to insure their students' success on the state assessment tests without having to do a whole lot more than follow along with the teacher's guides included with every box.

There was more money invested in the materials in that room than I had spent from my materials budget in ten years, and money was the wrong investment.

What the well meaning principal had done, out of desire to help the new teachers succeed in the high stakes testing environment, was unlikely to help them as teachers. He had put a barrier between three young energetic teachers and the opportunity for them to thoroughly invest themselves in their careers. There would be little or nothing of their spirit and energy required in their teaching. They would only have to provide the students with the books, the lesson plans and the other assorted materials that were being unwrapped in as many classrooms as there were administrators whose educational template is a list of curriculum standards.

And it should have ended better for Marguerite, an energetic, intelligent and creative woman who taught seventh and eighth grade English for five years in a similar suburban school. She was not in that room, on my last day, but she might as well have been.

As Marguerite tells it:

The hardest thing about being a first year teacher is the overwhelming feeling that you might fail. Administrators and the state standards stare you in the face and make you feel like you might not be able to do this. The funny thing is that if they would trust your judgment and let you experiment creatively with your lessons and make decisions based on your kids (not the state given bullet points, you won't fail. You can't. You're there for your kids, not the state and administrators.

In order to be successful, teachers need to have the freedom to adapt. Being able to make quick creative decisions helps the students, but it also helps the teacher to function positively. Teachers are often asked to change plans at a moment's notice, given new standards and objectives they have to use immediately, shown new technologies that they are expected to seamlessly incorporate in their lessons, etc. Being creative allows the teacher to be able to adapt to these changes and new tasks in a way that ensures a positive environment for the kids sitting in the seats.

I left teaching because the process in which teachers are being forced to present their material to their students is moving in a direction opposite to what works. Kids are inherently creative spirits, but my former principal once told me in a meeting, to "Take out all the 'fat' and unnecessary creative parts." That is asking the students to block what comes natural to them. It's damaging not only to their creative spirit, but to the learning process itself.

What It's All About

Who can sift though the vast reservoir of information that is available and decide which of it merits being absorbed and retained—used—in a practical sense? It is not enough to try to train an entire society to be well prepared to succeed on Jeopardy or be able to carry in an intelligent conversation at a party or with a stranger on an airplane. The education that is required to maintain a society as we know it is an education that allows people to survive on the level that they are capable of surviving, regardless of their economic and demographic circumstances.

People must be educated to function in society as it exists on a scale greater than just their own neighborhood. They need to be educated to understand what is going on around them as it relates to the big picture—they must be able to communicate globally—if not in language, at least in understanding. There is a generation of students whose needs are being inadequately served by a system that values quantity over quality—and insistence on measuring performance based on finite achievement as a goal rather than quality of life achievement based on providing for individual needs and individual abilities.

Investment in education is a term that brings to mind, naturally, money. We think in terms of the cost of education being in dollars—usually tax dollars—which tends to be an inhibiting factor. The term tax dollars brings to mind government, which brings to mind politics, which brings to mind the fact that politics and education do not mix. Making education part of a political agenda is anathema to the smooth flow of the education process.

The actual investment in education must be by educators, and the investment itself is not money. It is energy, spirit, desire, talent, ability, commitment and all the other things that teachers bring to the classroom every day.

Remember the earlier statement that "The journey is more important than the destination?" People who believe that data is the critical factor in assessing the journey assume that the assessments themselves are the destination and that is where the success of education is measured.

In order for data to be valid, it must clearly define what is being analyzed. Most school grades are predicated on testing, that reflects, mostly, right vs. wrong. Therefore, it tends to dismiss the value of what is learned on the way that may not show up on the assessment tool.

We must not be so intent on determining right and wrong—passing and failing—as measures of success that we invalidate the progress of the learning—that we dismiss the possibility of right vs. "needs work."

We must maintain the philosophy that all students are *on the way to being right*, and it is up to us to finds a means for them to get there. We must provide a means for students to succeed. We cannot guarantee success, of course, but if we determine the direction that students need—their "learning channels"—then we are better able to point them in the right direction.

And the Secret Is...

I have been asked, periodically, what the secret to good teaching is. I don't have the answer to what *the* secret is, because there is no single technique, no single style, and no single talent that makes good teaching. I know that at the time I became a teacher, I was technically unprepared as far as current theory on education. I was "unlearned" as far as classroom techniques or philosophy, But I was well prepared in terms of ability to think and act under pressure, to adapt to change, to react.

These are things that cannot be taught, but develop only through experience and are fueled by some natural instinct toward teaching. Instinct and innate ability cannot be taught. They can only be brought to the surface and honed by practice and experience.

A handy distinction to make is that some students need teaching, some need coaching, some need encouraging and some are best if left to their own devices (with a little supervision). Clearly, it is a challenge to figure out which is which, and that's what we do, every day.

Still looking for THE secret? It can be as simple, or as hard, as this: **As the Zen master said to the hot dog vendor:** *Make me one with everything.*

The Missing Piece

What It's All About

How'd I get here?
I ask myself that a lot,
when I'm thinking about
things I could have done
with my life.

If I could have hit a curve,
for example,
and been a little taller,
and a step faster,
I could have been playing ball on TV
and making the big money.

Or if I had hung in there
with law school,
I could have been a judge by now
or a senator,
or at least a partner in a firm,
and making the big money.

But instead I walked
into a school when I needed a job,
and once I caught on,
I could have been a principal,
or maybe even a superintendent,
and making the big money.

But, instead, I'm in a classroom,
with a hundred and twenty kids
passing through every day,
trying to give them something that's
not about making the big money.

It's about when a conversation begins:
I had this teacher once....

                     Herm Card
                    The Poetry of Teaching, 1998

CHAPTER FIVE

THE ACT OF TEACHING:
activities and applications

The Reality of "Reality"

Teacher pre test:
Consider the following questions, and respond

- What is "reality?"
- What is your students' reality?
- How does their "reality" affect their performance (primarily) in the classroom?
- Is this ever a problem?

If you are worried that your answers are right or wrong, welcome to part of your students' reality.

Given the number of possible interpretations of the word "reality," it becomes increasingly difficult to use the word comfortably in conjunction with classroom learning assignments. "Perception is reality" is a concept that is very effective for baseball umpires, but is not so great for students.

Students' perception is skewed by their exposure to media and societal interpretations of what is "real," and by the incessant reference to elements of our society that are certainly not what most right-thinking humans see as reality.

Students often perceive reality to be solely reflected in others' experiences, talents or achievements. This makes them highly susceptible to frustration and failure when their own achievements do not stand up to the comparison. If students are constantly comparing themselves to others, they are not developing as individuals and therefore, not as learners. They merely become mimics, unable to recognize and develop their own sense of self and the importance of their own learning

Even though we are seldom in a situation where we can totally individualize instruction, it is important to understand the need to allow students to have input into their own learning. We recognize that students have unique learning styles, and they are generally aware of that as well. While we are aware of this through analysis and observation they are aware of it instinctively. If we ask students how they learn best, they will be able to respond intuitively. They will tend to respond that they learn better by "being told," by "being shown" or "by doing."

We put labels on these learning styles, but it is more important that we simply understand that they exist and teach accordingly. By encouraging students to think for themselves, and by providing activities that encourage them to explore the world around them, we are better able to produce learning activities that are realistic and relative, rather than just reflexive busy work.

The student who cannot relate to the assignment will be discouraged easily, and will not willingly enter into the learning process. By providing the student an opportunity to relate to the subject matter, we also provide him/her with the opportunity to succeed.

The activities that follow are all proven winners. They were created for use in an ELA environment, but all have been modified, adapted and effectively used by K-12 teachers in all areas of the curriculum. Think of them as basic ingredients to which you can add the necessary components to make the finished product your own.

ACTIVITY 1: *The Medium And The Message: Non-Traditional Publishing: the end of the "same old, same old."*

Most of us crave recognition for work well done, regardless of the type of work. Students need to see a relationship between their effort and the results. Grades are not the results that satisfy the "self"—they are, realistically, designed to satisfy the system. Students need to be recognized for their academic efforts just as athletes or musicians are. This activity is designed to provide that opportunity, and allow students to receive attention similar to that which is common to other performance-oriented areas of the school community

Performance opportunities for student-writers are limited, since writing is not a public activity. Usually, student written work is displayed on bulletin boards, part of a large black and white display, one after another, year after year. There is little to separate one from another except, perhaps, the grade a teacher has affixed to it. Publishing student work is a vital aspect of success in any cross curricular writing program.

Since traditional means of in-school publishing create a sense of "sameness" about the work, By creating a variety of publishing options, the students become involved with the piece on an additional creative level. The likelihood that they will care about the piece increases as it becomes artistic in a visual as well as verbal sense.

Students' investment in their writing increases with the prospect of "going public" with it. They realize that their work is going to be displayed and stand on its own merits. There is pride attached to such presentation, and this is a great opportunity to instill some of the legitimate self esteem that we strive for. Even today, I can look at 15-year-old photos of smiling students with their work and sense the pride they felt in the accomplishment.

The "non-traditional" publishing process is generally multi-genre. While there is the necessity for students to perform in specific genres in certain subjects areas, there is no reason to restrict the genres totally. By allowing flexibility—choice—at various times, by allowing students to work in comfortable genres is likely to also provide the opportunity for them to produce better work than they might if assigned to a strict genre at which they may find extreme difficulty. While limiting writing to that specific genre may ultimately improve their work in *that* genre, why not allow them to improve their learning in the specific subject are first?

This variety infuses a different energy into the process. The student becomes conscious of a relationship between the craft of writing and the artistry of the whole. This is an important distinction for students to make—it puts their work on multiple levels and enhances the artistic sense they have, or should have, toward their work and it creates the opportunity for them to succeed—to enhance their *earned* self esteem.

To begin, students must create finished writing. The second part of the project is for the students to determine and create an appropriate publishing medium for their work—writing first, medium second.

Generally the medium should not direct the writing. Tailoring the writing to the medium can tend to create stereotyped rather than creative work. For example, if the student decided he or she wanted to burn the written work into wood, a rather tedious process, it is likely that the written work would be short. This forced editing would most likely detract from the potential strength or message of the written work.

On the other hand, if the students have in mind a particular medium where their written work will ultimately reside, that medium may positively guide the creation of the written work if the student is able to establish a meaningful relationship between the written work and the display piece. A written work about a dog, pasted on a hockey stick, for example, would lack the thoughtful connection for which I strive, whereas a written work about vanity, printed on a mirror with red lipstick, ties the medium to the written work perfectly.

By making such a connection, the student's awareness of such things— the connection that can be made between the two media encourages and enhances multi-level thinking. Caring about the work creates a need and/ or desire to make both good. Why put bad writing on a good piece of art, or *vice versa*?

Although the publishing media might not always be greatly artistic, there is artistry required to create an interesting and appropriate context for the writing. The artistic stimulation creates a sense that the writing is somehow artistic—a creative endeavor rather than just a mechanical one. The students engage in artistic thinking in determining how to approach the publishing method, as well as engage in using various forms of technology to create the finished product.

As part of the process, I give the students a list of possible media on which to display their work. They are allowed to do as much or as little with the art part as they wish, but they need to reflect solid effort if the grade (alas, a major project needs to be graded) is to be a good one. I make no distinction between a medium that a student has created himself or herself, versus a medium that may have been commercially purchases, as long as the connection between the writing and the medium reflects logical and artistic connection. The connection may simply be that the medium enhances the appearance of the written piece.

There is a clear opportunity for cross curricular application of this assignment. For example, physical education students might attach reports to an appropriate sports related medium. History reports could be printed on paper that students might have "aged" by painting it with tea. The scope of such projects would depend on the imagination of students and teachers.

Of course the medium itself make not make the report any better, but it will most likely make the student more connected to the work and willing to put more significant effort

Suggested "Old School" Media

Writing in a Bottle (or can or jar or box or...) Create a container for the written work with that may contain the written work or have the written work affixed as a label. The writer decorates the container, perhaps including a picture and biographical sketch of him/her.

- *CD Jewel Cases*: A jewel case may be used to display the writing as well as decoration, such as a picture of the writer, biographical sketch, or written work-related theme. It can be displayed standing up like a picture frame.
- *Writing Scrolls*: Writing may be done on long rolls of paper (fax or adding machine paper will do nicely if you can find such things anymore) to create a long class compiled work, or a display filed with short individual works. Short scrolls may also be created for individual pieces, and then given an aged effect by soaking in tea, then being rolled and tied with ribbons. This technique is particularly effective for history related topics.
- *Carved Writing*: Short pieces may be carved or burned into wood scraps, then shellacked or varnished for display.
- *Magnetic Writing*: Written works may be printed on special magnet-backed paper, and then displayed on metal backing. There are also business card sized magnets available that are ideal for short written works, especially haiku. (Both types of display can them be taken home and displayed as refrigerator magnets.)
- *Packaged Writing*: Pieces may be printed on paper which can then,

using an Ellison Cutter convert the piece into its own package—box, bag or whatever shape might be chosen. It can then contain a gift or *be* the gift.

- *Choose Your Own*: Students are encouraged to create their own medium, (with teacher approval) thus making the learning and the activity the finest example of connecting with both the written product and the artistic presentation.

This last choice often results in some spectacularly clever art.—a girl whose hobby is making beaded jewelry, bent wire and added beads to create the words in her fourteen line poem. A boy's memoir about playing the violin was applied with decoupage onto a carved violin, and a girl's poetry about her struggles with ballet (cleverly titled *What's the Pointe?*) appeared inside one of her ballet pointe shoes.

The project creates a wonderful sense of energy and accomplishment, even among students who might not always be actively engaged in their learning.

Twenty-First Century Publishing.

Over the course of the 16 years that I used this project in my classroom, technology evolved significantly, making the artistic part of the process easier and more "user friendly" for the students. Since I retired in 2006, even more evolving technology has created an entirely new professional publishing environment. The increased reliance on technology in the publishing world results in an extensively increased menu of publishing options and gives students an increasing ability to utilize an amazing variety of options

The increased emphasis on technology in schools provides a variety of options to record and disseminate information.

Even when away from school, the availability of Smartphone technology, for example, enables students to create video, photographic and audio recordings of most of what they experience, thus bringing an authentic research capability to their work.

By combining their own expertise with technology with the freedom to use it to publish their work, they are able to make even more connections between their learning and their lives.

Evaluation

Regardless of the methods—high tech or low tech—- the effect is the same. A project of this type enables students to make a connection to their learning through utilizing their own talents and interests. They gain an appreciation for the fact that the life they lead is relevant to what they are learning—and very important—to the *way* they are learning.

By employing technology or media that is familiar to them, they are also able to grasp the concept that connects the ordinary routine of daily life to a larger concept—that daily life contains learning—that not all learning is done in school and that not all learning requires that they be taught something—self sufficiency in their learning leads to more effective and more successful learning.

Therefore, when the question of grading the project comes up, we must keep in mind that we are asking students to put an artistic and original spin on what is typically "just" academic work. Grading artistic work along with the academic requirement allows us to consider the key question of how much the student was actually engaged in the process of learning. If the students are aware that legitimate effort does, in fact, count, they will be far more willing to put forth the effort required to succeed. If we are clear that the better the connection between the written piece and the presentation, the better the grade result will be.

What's In It For Us?

> *Maybe for me it was about the student who turned in NO other assignments all year, who stood beaming with his poem—written on a cloth scroll, wrapped on hand carved handles, the cloth made to look old and weathered with holes burned in it, the poem about his wretched home life. He who would fail eighth grade, who would drop out before 9th grade, who would disappear from my sight but not my memory. The young man who would tap me on the shoulder five years later and shake my hand and remind me of his name and tell me that the only thing*

he had ever done in school that meant anything to him was to write a poem on a scroll in eighth grade because it was the only way he could ever say what he had to say.

Herm Card, 2013

SAMPLE ASSIGNMENT: This is merely one way to approach this project. Teachers should adapt the assignment to their own specifications, depending on grade, subject, curriculum or other relative factors. This is an ELA 8 project—easily adaptable to other grades and other subjects.

The Medium and the Message.

By the end of this part of our study of poetry, you will have created a number of finished (or almost finished) poems. To complete the project you must choose a poem you have finished.

The second part of the project is for you to determine and create an appropriate publishing medium for your work.

Below are a number of suggested media:

Package the Poem:
Create a container for the poem with a sealable can or jar-like container, which may contain the writing or have the writing affixed as a label. The writer would decorate the container, perhaps including a picture and biographical sketch of him/her.

CD jewel cases:
A jewel case may be used to display the writing as well as decoration, such as a picture of the writer, or related theme, as well as a biographical sketch of the writer. It can be displayed standing up like a picture frame.

Scrolls:
Poems may be written on long rolls of paper (fax or adding machine paper) to create a long class poem, or a display filed with short individual works. Short scrolls may also be created for individual poems, then given an aged effect by soaking in tea, then rolled and tied with ribbons.

Carved poetry:
Poems may be carved or burned into wood scrapes, then shellacked or varnished for display

Magnetic writing:
Poems or short writings may be printed on special magnet-backed paper, and then displayed on a metal object. There are also business card sized magnets available that are ideal for short poems, especially haiku. Both types of display can them be taken home and displayed as refrigerator magnets.

Poetry Pottery:
Poems may be etched into clay before glazing and firing.

TBA: Other ideas may be announced.

Choose your own:
Self-explanatory—but talk to me about it BEFORE you begin so that we can be sure it will be workable in the time frame we have.

NOTE: I must approve all poetry and project ideas in order to insure that they are workable and to avoid duplication.

REMEMBER: Grades will be based on the QUALITY of the finished product and the EFFORT put into it.

DUE: TBA—Remember, Projects will displayed as part of our celebration of National Poetry Month (April)

ACTIVITY 2: *There's More To A Scrapbook Than Just Scraps*

Since one of our goals is to create a legitimate relationship between our students and their learning, it is imperative that we craft a framework that is clearly based in their reality. Much of the current curricula have established a basic informational standard that bears little relevance to the day to day lives—and the future—of today's students.

Essentially, education is liberal arts based. A wide spectrum of information is presented to a student that is not so much a test of the quality of their learning, but as a test of their ability to retain facts. The intent of the liberal arts education has always been to create well rounded individuals, knowledgeable in many areas.

This is certainly an ideal outcome, but the downside is that it is becoming increasingly more difficult to convince students that what is being taught is important to them. If it's not important, why learn it? If it can't be made clearly relevant, they will not bother with it, and the more they don't bother with it, the more they won't bother with the system as a whole. We live in an era where instant gratification is the expected result on all levels and consequently students, and teachers, become impatient with the system.

Most curricula require the student to look outside of themselves to the extreme. Students need to look outside, but they must recognize, or at least relate to what is there. By establishing contexts that are clearly connected to the students, the more connected they will be to the act of learning—and the learning itself.

Overview

NOTE: *This was originally an ELA based activity, but can be expanded and enhanced to include all areas of the curriculum. By expanding it in that way, it creates learning possibilities that incorporate elements from all subject areas, thus enhancing the idea of interconnected learning. (Where it says "ELA," plug in another subject area and you will see the possibilities inherent in the activity.)*

In September, students will be introduced to the project. Over the course of the year in ELA, students will create individual scrapbooks that chronicle the year from their perspectives. The goal of the scrapbook project is to create a body of work, covering all the writing genres they will experience while they connect with the "real" world.

The scrapbook will involve a number of cross-curricular applications, and will reinforce the concept that all curricula interconnect. It will contain reflections of themselves as individuals and as members of the larger world community. They will engage in analytical thinking in order to determine the relationship between themselves and the various elements of their environment and society as a whole.

Through the year, they will be expected to acquire "scraps" of their world, through reading, writing, researching, interviewing and reflecting and as with a typical scrapbook, they will secure the bits and pieces collected in the book chronologically. Each "scrap" will be accompanied by written reaction or reflection on its significance.

They will be required to connect with the world through reading a variety of genres, doing authentic research through written and electronic media and personal interviews. They will record their findings through visual and written genres in their scrapbooks. The writing will be done in a variety of genres covering all those that are part of the grade level curriculum.

By using authentic research through connecting to elements of their environment, they will understand that *they* are their own best resource.

Student Development Goals through Creating the Scrapbook:

They will create writing inspired by the reality that surrounds them on all levels. They will improve writing skills in the genres studied and practiced in their ELA curriculum, and applying these skills in all other subject areas.

They will be better able to determine appropriate styles and types of writing for a given purpose and will come to understand the essential relationships among all subject areas that become relevant to this project.

They will enhance their ability to interpret primary documents through utilizing such common sources as newspapers, magazines, and broadcast news media.

They will increase their ability to analyze and write reflectively on information they obtain and enhance their ability to compare and contrast information gleaned from a variety of sources.

They will improve their reading comprehension through exposure to a variety of genres.

Evaluation

Evaluation/assessment should be an ongoing process throughout the year. The written content of the scrapbook can be evaluated in the traditional manner for grading writing, as well as for its subject area content. Additionally, it will be evaluated on the basis of effort, depth of thinking, originality and variety of content, and the overall quality of the ongoing and finished product.

Consideration will be given to the depth of thinking and originality involved in the selection of the "scraps" of their life and society that they select. Likewise, the required "decoration" of the scrapbook will be considered as an essential part of the process. The evaluation will not be on the artistic quality to a degree that it will penalize less artistic students, but will be based on the connection made between the visual and written elements.

They will also be evaluated on their engagement in the process, taking into consideration their effort and the overall quality of the final product.

As with all activities of this type, assessment is somewhat holistic, based on a number of factors applied to individual student achievement, rather than to the group as a whole.

Since it is a yearlong project, students will have opportunity to continually revise and improve the product, thus improving their ability in revision/editing skills.

Notes on the Process

I employed this as a year-long activity that replaced the typical writing folder that we used to keep track of student writing. The scrapbook created and artistic tie to their writing and created a permanent record of their school year. Since the scrapbook never left the room, there was not likelihood of "lost work" and it was easily accessible.

The initial program was grant sponsored, but its success encouraged the principal to allow budget consideration.

Other than supplied items like construction paper, glue, scissors and some technology, students were responsible for the mechanics of creating and maintenance of the scrapbook itself. The required artwork was generally left to their own interpretation, creation and implementation.

The scrapbooks themselves were spiral bound in the school library, I scanned and printed copies of photos that parents did not want to lose.

Essentially, the writing was completed in typical fashion for the genre being used, up to the point of actually pasting it in the scrapbook. The due date for assignments was labeled "Scrapbook Day" and the period was devoted to cutting, pasting and sharing of work. The main requirement was that there is no mess left at the end of class.

Scrapbook Chronicle Overview for Students (Sample)

Assignment:

This year you will engage in a yearlong project, in which you will create a scrapbook of your year in (x) grade. This will not be a typical scrapbook—It will be one in which you will be continually making connections with the world around you, and turning these connections into writing in all the genres that we typically use..

- Much of the writing that you do for the year will be contained in this scrapbook, and it will be a major portion of your writing grade for each marking period and for the year.

- As the year progresses, you are encouraged to make connections to what is around you. You should begin to "notice" things that you might not ordinarily, on levels different from your usual connection. As you do, you should think about the significance of these "things" in terms of the effect they have on you and the world around you.

- These relationships will become the source of your writing, and you will be able to use the different types (genres) of writing that we study to create your responses.

- You will also discover the beneficial nature of this work in your social studies class, because you will be doing the same type of thinking that you are encouraged to do in that curriculum. There will also be entries which relate to other areas of the eighth grade curriculum

- You will receive a basic outline as to the content and process for creating your scrapbook that will be updated as the year progresses.

- You will create the book itself with materials provided, but you are free (and encouraged) to use your individual artistic and creative talents to enhance its appearance. You are NOT required to spend money on outside materials in order to enhance your grade. The appearance element of your scrapbook does not require anything other than imaginative application of effort. Commercial scrapbook materials will not, by themselves, improve your grade.

- You are encouraged to decorate the cover (in good taste) in a way that personalizes it—that is, makes it a reflection of you.
- The individual writing pieces contained in your scrapbook will be graded, and the book-to-date will be graded at the end of each marking period.
- As the year progresses, and as we have explored more genres, you will have more latitude (freedom to choose) as to the genres you employ for each assignment.
- You will be given assignments due on specific dates, but you will also have "wild card" entries that may be done at anytime during the marking period, as long as they are completed before the deadline.
- Some of your assignments will be very specific, others more general in nature. You will be given some assignments well in advance, while others might be homework type assignments relating to a current event. You will have sufficient time to prepare the writing and include it in the scrapbook. Much of this actual assembly will be done in class, after the work has been submitted and returned.
- *Examples* of the types of assignment you will be given are:

    **Find a newspaper article of significance on a state level and explain how it might affect you.
    **Write a poem inspired by a picture you find in the print media
    ** React to a quote by (your choice)
- As in most of your written work, your grade will depend on the quality of your written response, the quality of its relationship to the task, your engagement in the process, and the overall artistic quality of the product.
- You may produce your written entries in any form, but handwritten entries MUST be legible to receive credit.
- (For ELA students) As in the past, your final exam grade will take

- the form of a writing portfolio, so this scrapbook will enable you to have a great deal of writing to choose from in preparing the portfolio.
- Since you may want to use some of your scrapbook entries in your year-end portfolio, you should keep computer written entries in your SCHOOL computer file. If you wish to use handwritten entries in your portfolio, you will have to copy them at that time.

More information will be announced as the year progresses.

TEACHER NOTE: sample assignments

Scrapbook and Visuals

Items with # may be "renderings." i.e. they may be pictures similar to what you mean to be represented. Some items are underlined because of their importance.

- Select a photo# representing a sport or other skill activity that you do. Explain why you do it.
- Write a nature haiku or poem about the season# you like LEAST
- Write a letter to the editor about a local problem. Include a representation of the problem. (#photo, article, graphic, etc.)
- Find an article about education in the United States and respond to it (Think about how the subject of the article might affect you).
- Include a cartoon and explain why it is funny to you.
- Write an advertisement to persuade people to live in (your hometown).
- Argue (pro/con) an issue that is related to your school. It should be something that involves/affects you. Be sure you make your points clear.
- Explain the steps you will have to follow in order to have the career that you want.

- Write a letter to a public figure to try to get help in solving a problem that someone you read about (or saw) in the news is experiencing.
- Find some GOOD news in print. Write a letter thanking whoever made it possible.
- Write about your favorite performer. (actors, musicians, dancers, etc.). Explain why they are your favorite.
- Write about someone you respect OTHER than an athlete or performer.
- Include an advertisement. What does it NOT include that is important and probably left out intentionally. Explain why.
- Include favorite song lyrics or poem (in good taste—show them to me to approve them if there is ANY question). Explain their meaning and why they are important enough to be your favorite.

ACTIVITY 3: *Teaching with the Stars*

An important element in success at any activity is confidence—the knowledge that one is *able* to succeed at an endeavor. Students are typically so overly concerned for their immediate success that they lack the confidence required to succeed over the long term. Teachers can be disheartened by lack of success by their students. Confidence is important for both teachers and students if there is to be successful learning.

Remember the analogy of the baseball player who is successful if he/she bats .300—only a 30 percent "success" rate. Yet even faced with failing 70 percent of the time, players feel that every time they come to bat, they will succeed. The same applies to free throw shooting, ballet dancing, wood carving—people who expect to succeed, and understand what constitutes success, tend to succeed.

An important element in confidence is understanding what one is good at and what one needs to work on. Naturally, there are responses and results in school that are "wrong"—2+2 does not equal 3, for example, and even though that is close, it is not correct.

The essence of getting students on the path to being right requires that we instill in them a sense for being on that path. (Remember the Zen thing about learning taking place on the journey.)

We need to make them *aware* of themselves. No one is good at everything, or bad at everything. Students need a sense of safety—they need to able to fail constructively—profit from mistakes, not suffer because of them. A well known college baseball coach says that when he scouts a high school player, he wants to see the player make an error so that he can see what happens on the next play he has to make. A student who rebounds from a lack of success is on the path to "being right", while a student who accepts failure as inevitable, is not.

Our job is to assist them in rebounding, and instill in them the sense of confidence necessary for them to do so. Likewise, we must be confident enough in ourselves to give them the leeway to experience the success that should follow a less than successful outcome.

Confidence comes from a sense of understanding the self and what we are *realistically* capable of accomplishing. If, for example, we ask students to write a short autobiography—just a few lines to describe themselves, hardly any of them will pick things that they are not successful at. They will probably include some data to support their success. They will not define themselves introspectively. Neither will we if we ask ourselves the same question. But, in order to succeed, in order to become confident with ourselves, we must do just that—we must discover the things that work, and improve the things that need improvement.(or admit to) the things that need work.

Teaching with soft data

As teachers, we are too often prone to saying "I'm not good at that," and allowing that to prevent us from teaching certain things. For several years I taught poetry in a very perfunctory way because didn't "get it." But, when I began to write poetry, I realized there was nothing overwhelming about it. I have worked with many teachers who shared their fears at doing a particular type of subject matter but eventually became quite successful at teaching it. Get started by filling out the *Factors of Teaching Success* (see Chart #1).

Doing this teacher activity enables you to take a look at yourself in terms of how you perceive success. It may give you some insight into your expectations for your students and yourself and to be able to separate what we are *told* indicates success and what we *know* indicates success.

There is no rubric or answer key for it, so you may want to do it more than once during the year. One of the best district administrators I ever worked for had a term for it—"soft data." It is simply a way to use your own perceptions regarding the way things seem to be going.

Timing Is Everything

These activities are best done early in the year, since the result of the student work will provide you an awareness of their perceived strengths and shortcomings and allow you to address these issues through your teaching. You will move into the school year equipped with information about their skills that they have provided you,

Logically, why would you want them to become aware of elements to improve their learning at the *end* of the year? Why would you not want to have an entire school year to help them succeed through maximizing their skills and improving the areas that need work? Why would you not want the chance to improve your awareness of yourself as a teacher?

Rhetorical questions, for sure.

Activities

We tend to think of ourselves as teachers in a rather narrow view—as if there is a part of us that is a teacher, another part as a parent, another part as a runner, another part as a pianist, etc. It is all these things that make us able to each of them. So teaching is really an element of our lives that relies on all the other elements to thrive.

By doing these exercises along with our students, we are able to understand the connection between our personal traits and the things we do professionally and in our "other lives."

The point of the exercises is not to merely accept personal traits as being the determining factor in our success, but to be introspective enough to utilize them to our advantage.

The following activities are designed to create an awareness of self, separate from the numbers—the data—with which we so often identify.

The results should give us some important insights into our students and ourselves.

There are two activities that follow. You may use both, or choose the one that best fits your style and energy and that of your students. Regardless of which you choose, there is a corresponding activity for you to try out. Do it first in order to gain a sense of what the students will experience.

The specific responses are unimportant. What matters is the awareness that comes from the analysis.

Autobiographical Sketch

Too often, we tend to perceive themselves in a data based sense—we claim to be "more than a number," but have difficulty getting away from our data-driven culture.

Students, in particular, associate themselves with measurement, because they are constantly confronted with the need to achieve numerical benchmarks.

The following activities are designed to create an awareness of self, separate from the numbers—the data—with which we so often identify. The results should give us some important insights into our students.

Teacher Activity

You should first try this out on yourself, then adapt it to use in your classroom in a way that fits your particular methodology.

- Write an autobiographical sketch—a basic description of you. Do it in two or three paragraphs. Think of it as something that you might be using on a resume or a membership application or an item for your college alumni bulletin.
- Put it away for a day.
- Examine the elements in it that relate to data—things than could be measured and put on a graph, or could be used to relate achievement to a standard or to other people. It is unlikely that you would be unable to find such things.
- We relate to data because we are used to comparisons. As adults we have a great deal more to compare than our students do, and we are

better able to understand the significance, yet we can still be guilty of such.

- Take one of the items that is clearly related to data. Let's say you have written "I was a dean's list student in college." That is clearly data based because it required a certain GPA for you to make that list. But that is not introspective—is just a fact.

- Remove that fact from the context and finish this statement: "I was a dean's list student in college *because*...."

Once you are required to explain your data based item, you have to become introspective—you have to identify the traits you possess that enable you to excel. You might say that you studied hard, wanted to make your parents proud, wanted to get a good job, or any number of other reasons that reflect on you, rather than the data. Data is related to cause and effect. The data might be the effect, so what is the cause?

What this will do for your students is allow them to understand that there is more to them than just results—*They are not the data.*

As adults, we are more aware of the factors that follow "because," and less likely to be surprised at the revelation. So, if a student were to write "I am a B student in social studies," what introspection could come of that? What could we, as teachers, learn from it?

If the response was something like "I am a B student in social studies because I work really hard," we understand that the student is aware of limitations and is proud to be overcoming them.

"I am a B student in social studies because I am lazy," suggest the student is aware that he/she has ability that isn't being used. "I am a B student in social studies because I don't like school," shows another interpretation, as does "I am a B student in social studies because I have a hard time reading," or "I am a B student in social studies because it is boring." Each of these responses has information that is important to us as educators in that they give us insight into our students.

Student Activity

- Write an autobiographical sketch. (Teacher note: It will helpful to have the class brainstorm to understand that an autobiographical sketch is a condensed autobiography and create a list of items that should/could be included in such a piece.)

- Identify any items in the piece that relate to data (numbers, scores, percents, grades, etc.) and underline them.
- Pick one of the items, write it out again, add the word "because" and finish the sentence.
- Explain how the new version is a better example of "who" you are.

Evaluation

This is not an activity that should necessarily result in any type of grading, other than being considered as a completed assignment. Its primary use is as a means for students to engage in some introspection that validates the fact that they should view themselves in relationship to how they perform regardless of how others perform or evaluating themselves solely on numbers.

Teaching With Your Horoscope (see Chart #2)

Keep in mind that we are not suggesting that students or teachers believe in astrology or in zodiac signs. We are simply providing an organized opportunity to select a few traits that they feel they possess and some that they feel that they don't. They will be examining the traits to evaluate the things about themselves that work well and things that don't. The effect of the exercise is to demonstrate to students a means for being introspective—a means to examine their own characteristics and use the knowledge of themselves to their advantage.

Regardless of subject area, students' awareness of individual characteristics can be used to enhance their means to succeed. By filling in the information in the chart, the students create for themselves a base of material to analyze, apply to themselves, and then consider how each characteristic might help or hinder them in their learning.

As in the previous activity, teachers should do this one first in order to get a sense for how the students will experience it.

Teacher Activity

This requires no explicit belief in astrology or the zodiac. It's simply a way to allow us to focus on traits that we may possess that have an effect on our teaching. It encourages introspection and self analysis, with the goal of strengthening our resolve and affirming our awareness that we are doing the right thing for the right reasons.

By focusing on the skills we possess, and by understanding their effect on our work, we are better able to channel our energies in a positive direction. Teachers are frequently as guilty as students in comparing themselves to other teachers rather than being secure with their own abilities…

We accept that students learn through multiple intelligences, so we must likewise accept that we teach through multiple intelligences. By understanding the traits that affect our teaching, we are better able to direct our flow of teaching energy in the proper channel. While we may be aware of our strengths and weaknesses in teaching, it is difficult to define them. To know that it is difficult to do something does not necessarily direct us to a means for improving it rather that doing something else.

I was the poster boy for fear of teaching poetry for many years. I was not comfortable teaching it because I "didn't get it" in an artistic or intellectual sense. I only became a decent poetry teacher when I began writing poetry and reading poetry and began tom understand that the essence of the genre was far less intimidating than I had thought.

I realized over time that being (like my fellow Cancers) "introverted, reserved, emotional, sensitive, sympathetic, security-conscious, prudent, retentive, domestic, protective, quiet, calm, imaginative, conscientious, moody and traditional," was not necessarily something that should inhibit my abilities as teacher, poet, or anything else. I understand that a lot of other things that might show up on a different zodiac chart as well, but the point is that by analyzing these traits I am able to understand that it is not the trait that determines the outcome, but the adaptation of the trait—the application of it—that enabled me to succeed.

- Find the Zodiac sign that corresponds to your birthday.
- Read the character traits that are listed. Be sure that you understand what each of them means.
- On the chart, list the traits that you feel apply to you in one column (Similar) and the ones that don't in the other (Different).

- Examine your "similar" list and decide the ones that are MOST like you.

- CIRCLE the ones that contribute to your success in ANY way. (not just school)

- UNDERLINE the ones that can cause problems for you.

- For each one, explain WHY you made that decision—how do they relate to you?

Student Activity: (see Chart #3)

You do not have to believe that astrology or zodiac signs are real. This is just a good way to help you make a list of some of the traits (characteristics) that you possesses that can help you succeed at whatever it is you might be doing.

- Find the Zodiac sign that corresponds to your birthday.

- Read the character traits that are listed. Be sure that you understand what each of them means.

TEACHER NOTE: The method for insuring that students understand the meaning of the traits can vary according to your classroom procedure. It can be accomplished through class discussion of the entire chart as you introduce the lesson or through such things as looking them up or through discussion in writing groups.

- On the chart, list the traits that you feel apply to you in one column (Similar) and the ones that don't in the other (Different).

TEACHER NOTE: During this part of the process, it is best if students work alone to insure that their decisions are based on their individual perceptions of themselves and not influenced by others opinions.

- Examine your "similar" list and decide the ones that are MOST like you.

- CIRCLE the ones that contribute to your success in ANY way. (not just school)

- UNDERLINE the ones that can cause problems for you.

- For each one, explain WHY you made that decision—how do they relate to you?

Evaluation

As with the previous activity, this is not intended as "gradable" work, since it is designed to alleviate concern over the reliance on data. Note the similarities between the traits you list as positive and as challenging on your teaching list and your student list

It is logical that the traits that you list as positive contribute greatly to making you an effective teacher. However, you may also notice that some of the "challenging" traits also make a significant contribution by forcing you to adjust your attitude, style or thinking in such a way as to overcome them. This creates teaching strategies that not only overcome your challenges, but quite likely address some of the similar challenges facing your students. Students with challenging traits make us work harder, and working harder frequently makes us work better if we are focused on the elements of the work

This is "soft data." If you help a "challenging" student improve, data (numbers) is only the surface indicator…the quantitative factor, not the qualitative factors that truly reflect improvement by the student and by you.

If you still want an actual product, try the bumper sticker activity that follows. This will allow everyone, including you, to put this activity to practical use.

CHART #1

Factors of Teaching Success

What factors of teaching success ARE quantifiable? (can become DATA)	What factors of teaching success ARE NOT quantifiable? (cannot become DATA)

Write your definition of teaching success:

CHART #2 | **Teaching with the Stars**

Use a horoscope chart (a sample is at the end of the chapter) to determine the trait(s) of your sign that are positive and those that challenge you. List them and explain.

Circle the ones that make you an effective teacher. Don't be surprised if some are in the "challenging" column.

Positive Traits	Negative Traits

Explain how your circled traits contribute to your being a good teacher.
Be sure to consider the "challenging" traits, as well.

CHART # 3

Learning with the Stars

Use the horoscope chart to determine the trait(s) of your sign that you think fit you, and those that don't. List them below, pick the **most** similar and different, and explain how and why they fit and don't fit you.

Similar	Different

Begin your draft here, continue on the back.

Make a "data-free" bumper sticker that defines you as a teacher.

- Create a bumper sticker that removes the sense of data as an indicator of achievement. It should reflect
- your teaching success in terms of your own goals and accomplishmentss. Decorate it to help make your point.

Post it somewhere that you will see it every day.

Student Bumper Sticker

- Create a bumper sticker that your parents might put on their car to 'brag' about you.

- Be sure that it doesn't have a sense of data, but shows a sense of your accomplishment and success in terms of *your own* goals and expectations.

Sample Horoscope Chart

Aquarius: January 20 - February 18
Aquarius is individualistic, unconventional, progressive, unique, independent, humanitarian, altruistic, visionary, perceptive, intellectual, logical, ingenious, inventive, unpredictable, detached, friendly, and scientific.

Pisces: February 19 - March 20
Pisces is receptive, supersensitive, impressionable, peace-loving, serious, sympathetic, charitable, compassionate, artistic, creative, dreamer, dedicated, imaginative, psychic, shy, introverted, spiritual, and reclusive

Aries: March 21 - April 19
Aries is energetic, innovative, original, pioneering, assertive, quick-tempered, strong drive, leader, ambitious, extroverted, sometimes aggressive, competitive, enthusiastic, self-reliant, and self-assured

Taurus: April 20 - May 20
Taurus is determined, efficient, stubborn, cautious, placid, persistent, enduring, introverted, conservative, conventional, materialistic, security conscious, stable, industrious, dependable, and one generally having significant financial ability.

Gemini: May 21 - June 21
Gemini is flexible, versatile, restless, a jack-of-all-trades, lively, alert, quick-witted, literary, communicative, a good conversationalist, changeable, sociable, logical, ingenious, agile, dexterous, intellectual, and mentally ambitious.

Cancer: June 22 - July 22
Cancer is introverted, reserved, emotional, sensitive, moody, sympathetic, security-conscious, prudent, retentive, domestic, maternal, protective, quiet, calm, imaginative, conscientious, and quite the traditionalist.

Leo: July 23 - August 22
Leo is ambitious, a lover of limelight, speculative, extroverted, optimistic, honorable, dignified, confident, proud, exuberant, sunny, flamboyant, charismatic, dramatic, competitive, a leader and an organizer.

Virgo: August 23 - September 22
Virgo is practical, responsible, sensible, logical, analytical, highly discriminating, a careful planner, precise and punctual, dedicated, perfectionist, critical, health conscious, and somewhat introverted

Libra: September 23 - October 22
Libra is idealistic, a peacemaker, diplomatic, refined, poised, gracious, kind, courteous, fair-minded, sociable, charming, artistically creative, affable, cooperative, extroverted, and usually somewhat indecisive.

Scorpio: October 23 - November 21
Scorpio is intense, determined, powerful, strong-willed, forceful, bold, courageous, enduring, competitive, resourceful, researcher, an investigator, secretive, mysterious, penetrating, psychic, self-reliant, and somewhat introverted or closed

Sagittarius: November 22 - December 21

Sagittarius is idealistic, optimistic, freedom-loving, casual, friendly, buoyant, gregarious, enthusiastic, philosophical, studious, farseeing, direct, outspoken, honest, loyal, restless and loves travel.

Capricorn: December 22 - January 19
Capricorn is ambitious (power, position, money), organizational, self-disciplined, rigid, thrifty, prudent, security-conscious, conservative, responsible, practical, persistent, political, business oriented, methodical.

Signs of Success

I have done my job
when the fist-pumping *Yeah!*
is the result of
a decent haiku.

And the extended
cooowullll
sneaks out of a writing group

and poetry books show up on the library's overdue list.

The Poetry of Teaching
Herm Card, 1998

ACTIVITY 4: *Learning Log*

One of the most important things to remember about dealing with new kids is that they may only be new to you.

Very early in my career, two of my students asked me if I had any harder work them. They were the two best students in my class and I knew that the work was probably too easy for them. I was probably a bit insulted that a student would question my curriculum, but mostly, I was surprised that students would want to be challenged.

Since I hadn't taken many classes that prepared me to teach, I wasn't totally able to deal with such a request. Ability tracking had recently come into disfavor, so there was no specific curriculum for better students. I was, essentially, stuck, not unlike the situation many teachers find themselves in today. Dealing with a diverse group of abilities tends to not meet the needs of most who do not fit the traditional bell curve. New kids understand this—they are intuitively able to realize when they are not being adequately served.

Unlike that student years ago, most are unwilling or unable to communicate this need. If students get As simply because they are A students, how are we helping them? An A student will probably be an A student despite us—but what learning will take place simply because excellence is a reflex with them, rather than something that must be achieved with hard work?

In order for students to have legitimate input into their learning, they must have the opportunity to analyze and react to it. By providing them a means to do so, we are able to engage them in cross curricular reading and writing as well as provide them a clear connection to their learning. Students have opinions about many things, but are frequently unable to express them because they have no platform to do so.

Feedback = Connection

If we value student input regarding what they read, why not value their input relating to what they are learning? Consider giving them the opportunity to actually react to what they are studying, rather than simply analyzing it. Providing them the opportunity to use a learning log can produce a number of valuable outcomes.

The activity will enhance their ELA skills through the writing activity, and provide the benefit of causing students to examine and react to the activities they engage in other areas of their curriculum.

Remember, we are trying to get them to connect to their learning—to understand its relevance and its overall value—reinforcing the idea that nearly all learning is cross curricular. This is reinforced as they see that even though the subject matter varies, they are using their thinking and reading and writing skills to bring their reactions to the surface.

As they become aware that they have input—that they are connected to their education—that they have a voice—they should see themselves as part of the process.

Of course, the activity can't become a free-for-all of "I like this" or "I don't like this" kind of response. Reacting requires legitimate thought. They need to understand that their reaction is a three part process. Stating an opinion with one or more reason to support it and an appropriate example makes the activity useful, not only to the student, but to the teacher as well.

A learning log is an excellent means to accomplish several things. By allowing students to react to the learning they are doing, we encourage them to actually connect themselves to it. By allowing them to analyze what they are studying and the means by which they are learning, we also receive valuable feedback as to how successful we are in reaching them.

Dealing with a generation of "new kids" in our classrooms, we find ourselves more inclined to question our teaching methods just as they are more inclined to question them as well.

By encouraging, and allowing students to be more involved in their learning, the better we are able to engage them in the process. The more we engage them, the better we are able tom teach them. The more they engage themselves, the more they will learn themselves. There is more success for them in the act of learning than there is in the act of being taught, They are more likely to succeed at making a connection not only to the material being taught in a specific class, but to material being taught throughout the curriculum.

Learning Log

Your learning log is a place for you to **react** to the learning you are doing. You do not simply explain what you have studied, but express your feelings about it. You can react to facts, activities, things you learned, things you want to learn, the way you learn best, even the way you want to learn. Anything that causes you to come to a conclusion or feeling about the learning is something for you to write about.

On the lines below, react to the learning you are currently doing. Be sure to include enough information to be clear about the point you want to make.

Remember:
Reacting involves giving your **OPINION**, along with a **REASON** for feeling that way, and an **EXAMPLE** to support or explain your opinion.

OPINION ⇒ **REASON** ⇒ **EXAMPLE**

ACTIVITY 5: "FIELD TRIPS": Connecting students to school

There Is a Major Difference Between Being AT School and Being IN School.

Students who show up, are *at* school, but a significant percentage of them are not *in* school. Simply attending school does not give them a reason to learn. The reason must be something to which the students can relate. The standard line that "you will need to know this" is insufficient. If students are convinced that school is of no use to them, they have no motivation to become engaged in the process of learning. This can apply to students on both ends of the spectrum. Students, who tend to do well on everything, regardless of interest it, will routinely engage in the process, but not the learning. New kids are especially prone to this, since they see no reason to learn what they already know. Those who experience little success in school will likely not engage in the process because they would prefer to accept the failing grade rather than the frustration of not succeeding at what they see as an irrelevant task.

The majority of students are in the middle—they want to do well, or at least well enough to pass, but only see connections between themselves and their education when the connections interest them.

Show, Don't Tell: make learning interesting

How can we attract students to the process of learning? By making them *want to learn about something*. In a broad sense, all learning is based on research. It begins with the question as to what the learner wants to know *about*. This is a common enough experience for students. Regardless of the classroom subject, they are constantly being put in the position of trying to figure out topics for reports, papers, essays, poems, etc. Even in the circumstances where they are given a subject on which to focus there is still the underlying question as to what to do with it.

Students tend to be literal in their thinking, so they tend to focus on the topic and fear that deviation will take them out of the realm of being *right*. The concept of being right or wrong is a daunting premise for students. Once students are comfortable with the fact that there are far more ways of being right than wrong in the learning process, they should be able to relax enough to tackle a "field trip" to discover something.

There are many ways to approach this—from the very literal walk in the woods to a simple indoor search. Regardless of the way it is conducted, the most important thing is to allow students freedom of choice and freedom of thought.

The difficulty does not so much arise from the lack of an idea, but from the inability to deal with the idea. Students tend to focus beyond themselves. They do not bring the idea close to themselves, or relate it to what is familiar. They tend to either look at an idea on too grand a scale, or attempt to oversimplify it to the point where it reduces itself to the literal level of a grocery list.

Given an object—an hourglass style egg time for example, a student might be stymied by the fact that he/she does not even know what it is. Provided enough basic information as to the purpose and function, the student might then reach the stage of not knowing what to do anyway. What *could* the object be? What *could* it do? How *could* the student relate to it?

The object itself should not be the focus of the learning. Students want to think in the literal sense. A report is *about* something. A poem is *about* something. Math homework is *about* something. Actually, the student work needs to be *about* learning.

I shared a lot of my own writing with my students and often let them in on the beginning of the writing process in order to demonstrate how the process worked as well as giving them a sense of working with me.

I wrote this poem in response to a demonstration I gave of entering the writing process through association with an object.

Dead Solid Perfect

In my classroom, in a beautiful 1930s building,
a seven foot wooden pole serves to open the windows.
I roll it in my hands, stare deep into the grain.
It might be a Louisville Slugger,
Model D115, 34 inches, 32 ounces,
Syracuse University branded on the barrel.

The Missing Piece

I stand at the plate, game tied, bottom of the ninth,
my heart pounding.
The All-American pitcher,
who last year cracked my rib with a fastball,
throws that same fastball,
waist high on the outside,
to the spot where my swing is just right.

The contact is dead solid perfect—
the nothingness of a ball hit on the sweet spot,
no sting, no vibration,
just the bat on ball sound of wood on leather,
a flawless marriage under the laws of physics.
A white-tailed rocket streaks toward the gap in right
the winning run on the way to the plate,
until the right fielder, at full sprint,
dives, changes the story,
as leather meets leather,
turns my heroics into his.

I stare into the distance,
everything out of focus,
my perfect moment cut short.
I rest my hands on my knees, remember
my mother would be ashamed if I swore,
my father would expect me to show some class,
inhale deep, to slow my heart,
turn toward my spot at third base,
and walk to the front of my classroom.

When I asked my students what I was writing about, NONE said that I was writing about a window opener. They determined that I was writing about:

- Baseball (playing, being a player)

- Frustration (almost a hero, almost won the game, almost got a hit, made a spectacular out)

- Irony (almost got a hit off pitcher who hit me last year, thought it was a hit and it was caught)
- Failure (me, team)
- Success (the right fielder, the pitcher)
- Destiny (wasn't supposed to win, wound up a teacher, was supposed to be)
- Bad luck(ball was caught)
- Self control (didn't swear, showed some class, kept anger in)
- Trick ending (walked to front of class)

Let them practice what could be called the *chain of ideas* process, where one idea leads to another as I did in my poem. The key to illustrating the process is preserving all the ideas as my students did from my poem.

Have them concentrate on a common object in the room that you know would be difficult to write *about*, such as the clock. Students will likely feel that it is difficult to write about a clock because they don't know anything about it. This is probably, in a technical sense, true. They don't know about the machine, its parts its design, its history, its inventor or how it works. What they know is unimportant. What they are inspired to think about is the key. What might it remind them of? Solicit some responses as part of class discussion.

Typically literal responses might include:

"School"

"Boredom"

"Next period's test"

"Waiting for class to be over"

"What I'm doing after school"

Remember that the responses are unique to the students who contributed them, but might also inspire others' thoughts. This is a demonstration of how the chain of ideas might work.

For any individual, the chain might be something more elaborate and in more depth. Essentially all object inspires writing will reveal an emotional attachment to the ideas inspired by the object.

Once you have demonstrated this as a class exercise, it is time to let them out on their own with it. The key here is to use enough varied objects to allow everyone in the class the opportunity to relate to at least one of them.

The Idea Buffet

I call this exercise the "Idea Buffet." Because it provides the students the opportunity to sample a number of interesting choices for writing inspiration. It requires a certain amount of patience and practice, but is worth the effort.

You should tailor the exercise to your class, based on available time and size. Given adequate preparation collecting an assortment of diverse objects, it is a highly effective thought-provoker. I generally suggest short writing responses in order to enable the students to create a satisfactory product fairly soon to demonstrate the effectiveness of the process. Once they have seen the success they can have, they are likely to employ this technique as part of any creative writing experience in any subject.

Student Activity
Directions:

The Idea Buffet

- *As you move around the room, you will be presented with a "buffet" of assorted objects.*

- *Experience them in as many sensory ways as you can, but* **do not taste them.**

- *While you do this, write down the ideas, feelings, sensations, emotions, etc. that come to you.*

- *You might not relate to every object—don't worry about that.*

- *When you are finished, go to your writing place and allow your notes to take written form.*

YOU MUST BE QUIET *throughout the exercise so that our reactions to an object do not influence the reactions of others.*

Do not feel that you must produce a finished piece, but simply produce something, which represents your responses to the items you experienced.

Teachers will find that the students will respond authentically to the exercise and will be able to turn the pieces they create into extended product, regardless of subject areas.

Taking it on the road: The cross curricular aspect.

The cross curricular aspect of this activity requires a little coordination. For teachers who teach ELA/Social Studies, for example, it is easy enough to turn out extended lessons that cross over from one to the other. Team teachers can likewise extend the exercise, as appropriate to fit the schedule.

Time is not relevant in this case—the introduction done in one class prepares the students for the activities in the other, so the transition is not difficult.

In junior high situations, the coordination is simply a matter of implementing appropriately after the beginning session(s) have been conducted.

It's probably a bit optimistic to think that any given activity will inspire all students to excel, or even become interested in the learning. But, the more opportunities they have to connect to SOME part of the learning, the better chance they have to succeed at SOME part of their education.

Let's pretend we are in an elementary class. Let's further pretend that we are the math/science teacher or perhaps the ELA/Social Studies teacher—common combinations in elementary school. Let's further consider that we are trying to inspire students to learn—and in so doing, create a curiosity on their part. Also to utilize our time in a way that illustrates to them that a learning experience is seldom self-contained—that what they learn in one area can apply to others—that learning is not mutually exclusive or narrow and that they should not leave ELA at the door when they walk into science, math or social studies.

ACTIVITY:

Display an object that your students will recognize. It is irrelevant that they have any more connection than that.

For the purpose of my demonstration, I usually use a baseball. Nearly everyone will recognize a baseball. But suppose a student is new to America and has no idea what it is specifically. It is still a ball—something that very few cultures are without.

This baseball, for example, might seem to have only a physical education connection to many, but that is not the case. You should use an object of your own choosing that you are confident will work with your students.

Sample Activity

Put a baseball on the table in front of a class. Whatever the class doesn't matter. That's right—the class doesn't matter. It doesn't matter because the object itself is universal in its essence. It can be utilized as a teaching tool in nearly all subject areas of nearly any curriculum in nearly any school. The only requirement is to find an object that clearly relates across the curriculum.

The baseball, for example, is a generally familiar object that would most likely elicit the response—"That's just a baseball." But, when asked how it could be used in different subjects, the replies *should* lead to a variety of thoughts. That thinking in itself is pretty good practice for students to think outside the door of your classroom and prove that there is a connection among all subjects they are taking.

Ultimately the activity should result in the students coming to the understanding that they are surrounded by opportunities to learn through things that are familiar. They will come to understand that they are capable of undertaking their own learning—that school is not the source of learning, but that they are.

The demonstration object itself is up to the teacher (s) involved. The only requirement is that it relate to all the classes involved. It is not necessary for all subject areas to be involved—there is sufficient overlap to make the cross-curricular point since they will automatically need to involve other subject areas in the exercise. Math and science are not exclusive of each other, just as no subjects are exclusive from ELA

Typical applications using a baseball as the object:

SUBJECT	POSSIBLE APPLICATION
ENGLISH	memoir, report, poetry, reaction, journal, sports report, editorial, sports writers, biographies, fiction (about), non-fiction (about), literature, author
MATH	size, weight, shape, geometric shape
SOCIAL STUDIES	reports, history, sociology, economics, civil rights geography, biographies
SCIENCE	weight, velocity, mass, Trajectory, coefficient of reciprocity, composition
ART/MUSIC	painting, photography, collage, sculpture, clay, songs, singers
HEALTH/ PHYS. ED.	nutrition, fitness of athletes, rules, strategy, techniques, benefits, injuries, steroid and PED abuse and effects
TECHNOLOGY	multimedia applications, computer skills
OTHER	language classes could investigate sports in other countries; "specialty" classes, such as electives or independent study might connect in a variety of ways

Not only is it important to convince students that education is cross curricular, it is important for educators to understand the same thing.

It is likewise necessary to make them understand that what is part of class is also part of life, that they can learn from what they are familiar with; that things they know can teach them things they can apply to other learning.

We are in a time of limited budgets, limited resources and limited opportunity for teachers to infuse their classrooms with energy that translated into connections to the reality of the world in which their students live.

ACTIVITY 6: *If Socrates Hosted Jeopardy*

One of the keys to the success of *Jeopardy* has always been the unusual way in which the contestants' knowledge is tested. Just as in schools, most quiz shows rely on asking a question and having the contestant attempt to answer it. The *Jeopardy* concept, on the other hand, gives an answer and requires for a response that takes the form of a question. So it is with the essence of Socratic discussion using questions to reveal answers and encouraging the process as a means for extending the learning process beyond the simple teacher/student relationship.

Because new kids can tend to see their thinking as the right way (and the only way) becoming involved in debates can encourage them to see other's viewpoints. A well structured and monitored debate can allow them to express their opinions and at the same time, learn to consider other perspectives.

A concept to consider that addresses both critical thinking and analysis is based on the Socratic method of teaching. Greek philosopher/teacher Socrates approached education by allowing students to learn rather than having them feel they are simply being taught. This approach provides unique opportunities for analysis and reflection and enables students to be confidently involved in their own learning.

If Socrates were to make a statement that contained a widely held belief, he would then encourage students to question the validity of the statement in order to arrive at its ultimate truth. By encouraging students to question—to think, debate, inquire and examine various viewpoints, they become more engaged in the process of learning.

Thus, the *Jeopardy* approach, providing an answer that provokes questions, enables students to ponder the "fact" that is offered in a variety of ways, many of which can be "correct" in an educational sense.

The students use logic and methods of deduction to either support the belief or find contradictions. They are then instructed to persuade the members of the class to accept their conclusions. Of course, questions need to be appropriate to the students' level of ability and social development.

Because the questions students ask are based on legitimate speculation and curiosity rather than being on being right or wrong answers, students get to use their own methods of reasoning without the fear of being incorrect.

This method turns partial control and direction of the class to the students, encouraging them to work together and filling the need to be involved in their education.

This approach is in large part, based on Socrates' belief that new knowledge is based on prior knowledge and that thinking comes from asking questions rather than memorizing information provided for students. (remember, he was a new kid of his time)

Students need to be encouraged to ask questions in order to further their learning. They must also learn that simply asking questions without a focus is ineffective.

Once they are engaged in discussion on a topic, they should be allowed the latitude to progress through the process through constructive questioning and a search to verify that the things they perceive as facts actually are factual.

They must be open to the fact that they may not be right simply because they want to be right or feel that they are automatically right. They need to be encouraged to understand that there is usually more than one side to an issue, and by accepting this, they are on the way to discovering that the truth of an issue is quite often in the middle ground between two opinions.

Sample Activity

By creating hypothetically factual situations on which to base the questions. the teacher can control the direction of the exercise and establish answers that can be arrived at by a variety of means and through a variety of thinking processes.

Either through a class brainstorming activity or through individual contributions generate a series of questions that relate to the statement. The initial statement does not necessarily have to be factual or even logical, depending on the grade level.

Since the reality, is created based on the teacher's presentation, there is no requirement for "outside" knowledge that might prevent participation by students who do not have that knowledge. This also decreases the likelihood of the cultural bias that is an inhibiting factor in many learning (and testing) situations.

For example, reading the fable *The Tortoise and the Hare* would establish a seemingly logical context for the premise that turtles are faster than rabbits.

Clearly, there are logical and fact based arguments that would refute that. The exercise, however, requires the students to ask questions to prove or refute the premise, based only on the fable's information, rather than simply refute it through common knowledge. On *Jeopardy*, no one ever argues with Alex Trebek, but what student would pass up a chance to prove a teacher wrong? Of course, we are looking for a more mature exchange that simply asking "why" to every statement that is made, or to simply say that "Everybody knows that rabbits are faster."

Thus, from the outcome of the race in *The Tortoise and the Hare*, it would seem logical to make the statement that tortoises are faster than hares. (It might be helpful to point out that tortoises and hares possess the essential qualities of turtles and rabbits.)

Typical student questions might be:

Just because he won, is he automatically faster?
The hare was always ahead, how can the tortoise be faster?
Are turtles and tortoises the exact same thing?
Are rabbits and hares the exact same thing?
If tortoises are faster, why did he only win because the hare stopped?
What if the hare didn't stop?
Is being over confident always bad?
Why couldn't the rabbit figure out that stopping was bad?
Was the tortoise smarter than the rabbit?

Can being smarter make up for being slower?
Is one example of something enough to prove it is true?
Is there a point to the story that makes the tortoise seem faster?
And so forth.

Depending on the class level, the teacher can turn the activity into class-wide debate pitting "tortoises" versus "hares" to prove who is faster, smarter, or more persistent than the other

Ultimately, it should become clear that there is a logical fallacy in believing something simply because it is presented as fact by an expert. It's true, for the most part, that everyone *does* know that rabbits are faster and that there is a moral to the story that is based on the anomaly of the race result.

The outcome? Students are encouraged to look for proof rather than simply accept "facts" as presented, and to have a voice in their learning by actively participating in it.

ACTIVITY 7: *Make Your Day Better.*

Go with the flow. There is an inevitable ebb and flow of the energy of a school. Though we may not be able to totally control the students' energy, we can have a profound effect on our own. Arrive as early as possible, especially if you have homeroom or first period obligations. A silent school is peaceful It is full of years of positive energy and the silent moments before the students arrive is a perfect opportunity to absorb it.

Chaos Theory I

From chaos comes order
they say.

Were they thinking of
eighth grade when they said it?

Where is there more chaos
than in the world inhabited by
fourteen-year-olds?

Use this time to anticipate your day, but don't try to predict it. Predictions tend to direct the flow because we try to make them come true, which doesn't always work out. Anticipation allows for adjustment, predictions allow for disappointment.

Ritual

We gather, daily, in the morning light,
offerings in hand,
to seek his beneficence.

First in line, I shuffle forward,
whisper my self-conscious prayer
for his favor.

I place my offerings, tentatively,
on the cold,
hard altar.

As his words glow in the dim light,
I kneel, fearfully,
to do his bidding.

Clear paper jam in area 2
re-order originals,
then, press START.

Even though there is a constant starting and stopping throughout your day—one class ends, another starts—there is still an overall flow from beginning to end. Allow your energy to flow with it.

Chaos Theory II

From chaos comes order
they say.

The noise in the hallway
ebbs and flows as the traffic
reaches its peak
then subsides as they file into class
then picks up again
as they reacquaint themselves,
reliving the good times
and happy memories
of last period.

The success of any specific chunk of teaching is based on the teamwork between teacher and students. If a lesson doesn't work out, don't shoulder all the blame, but don't put it all on the students. A great activity one period might be less so with the next, or vice versa. Accept that nothing will work every time, but the things you do well work far more often than they don't.

Hypothesis

Is it possible
that I use chalk that is
not in the spectrum

of visible light
and speak in a voice that can't
be heard by students?

There's a saying that "If you want to make God laugh, tell him your plan." Trying to mold your day to fit a specific plan has great potential to cause you a certain amount of frustration. There are many things that can go wrong to make your well ordered lesson plan something of a shambles. However, just because something disrupts the flow of the lesson plan does not mean that it has disrupted the flow of the learning.

perfect lesson plan
great teaching a certainty
then came that fire drill

While the term "teachable moment" has become somewhat overused, the fact is that our days are filled with opportunities to offer something of value that was inspired by the moment, not the lesson plan.

Don't be too quick to dismiss what seems to be an off the track question or response. It may be off the track of your lesson plan, but possibly it is something you hadn't thought of. Trust that it is something the student needs, or just wants, to know. What may seem irrelevant to you might be a reflection of a different, yet legitimate, approach to the question. Of course, the downside is that since such a moment cannot be planned, it cannot be recreated in the same way next period. Don't try. Learn from it yourself. Find a way to include your insight at that moment into your teaching the next time you do that lesson. Thus, it has become a teachable moment for them and a "teacher-able" moment for you.

Idle Hands?

> He spent the better part of the period
> filling in the white spaces
> on the cover of his composition book.
> No wonder there was
> no time left to write the poem,
> though the silhouette of
> Emily Dickenson wasn't too bad.

Relieve yourself of the responsibility to know everything. Accept the diverse knowledge of your students. The increasing use and availability of technology results in many of our students being more knowledgeable and more proficient than we are. Don't be afraid to ask for help from them. What better moment can there be for a student who is able to contribute something to *your* knowledge, to help you learn, to make you better.

Good Advice

> It's really important
> that I not figure that
> I'm the intellectual giant in the room,

because when I do,
the odds are pretty good that someone
is going to prove me
wrong.

When my uncle would visit us from his home in New York City, he had difficulty sleeping because of the night time silence. It can be difficult for us to separate ourselves from the sometimes chaotic energy that surrounds us, but it is important that when we ask ourselves "What's that sound," the answer should be "Silence."

Chaos Theory III

From chaos comes order
they say.

My understanding of chaos
as it relates to education
is based on what occurs
at 2:21 every day.

You will find all the chaos
You could ever hope for
outside my classroom,
in the hallway,
at the lockers,
heading toward the buses,

and the only thing predictable
about this chaos
is that at it will recur
at 7:40 the next morning.

When the last student has gone, when the silence returns, reflect on your day. Ask yourself what you did to make your students better. Ask yourself what you did to make yourself better. You will *never* be able to correctly answer with "nothing," because the very act of reflecting makes you better, and if you are better, they will become better.

Remind yourself of the good you have done. This is no time for false modesty. It is a time for you to pat yourself on the back for what you have done. It is also a time to recognize that something might have been better, and to think about how to make it so. Introspectively, only you know what you have done that worked well, and what needs improvement. The idea of "learning on the journey" applies to you too, and these silent moments are an important part of your journey.

Chaos Theory IV

From chaos comes order
they say.

It is said that if a butterfly
flaps its wings in China,
it can cause a storm in Texas.

For over thirty years,
wings flapped in my classroom,

and chaos theory
played itself out for me
over and over again:

chaos, then order,
chaos, then order.

Storms, then rainbows.
Storms, then rainbows

Try to write down your thoughts. Write them however you want—prose, poetry, or shorthand scribbles. They are your thoughts, in your words. Keep in a journal, in your plan book, on note cards or wherever you will be able to look back and reflect on them, and be sure to do that reflecting. They are your thoughts on your day, but they will eventually be your thoughts on your life as a teacher.

End of the Day

Sometimes I find myself,
a little after three o'clock,
several minutes into my own time,
torn between
the desire to be somewhere else
and the joy of being where I am.

Poetry from *The Poetry of Teaching*[1] and...*or else it's only a job.*[2]

CHAPTER SIX

New and Selected Poetry from The Poetry of Teaching and ...or else it's only a job.

Thanks, Roy

In 1972, my friend Roy,
the head basketball coach
at Syracuse University,
(and that's a pretty good job)
told me how lucky he was
to be paid to get up every day
and do something he loved.

And for years I thought about that.
What a thing to be able to say,
to feel,
to believe.

Recently,
I saw him at a banquet.
He has retired from several things,
lives on a boat, plays a lot of golf.

And I have taken his place.
Not coaching basketball at Syracuse, of course,
but getting paid to get up every morning
and do something I love.

Dolores R. Card, Hermon R. Card

For Student Teachers

Tattooed, bearded,
pierced navel and tongue.
long hair,
spiked hair,
colored hair,
razored hair,
dredlocked hair,
corn rowed hair,
no hair.

Back in my day, need not apply.

You can't look like that and teach, young man.
You can't expect anyone to take you seriously young lady.
Just who do you think you are?

> *I'll tell you who I am…I am you.*
> *I am you when you were young,*
> *I am you when you were new.*
> *I am you who dared to be yourself,*
> *and show them it's OK to be themselves.*

Hey, wait!
I don't want you to be me
I don't want you to look like me
or act like me
or even care about me.

I just want you to be the future.

When I Got Good at It

Ten years of teaching
adjectives and verbs

The Missing Piece

and to not write run on sentences

had not really made me
any kind of teacher
but had made me
the guy who had to explain
to the bored eyes and empty faces
why we had to do this and what the point was
and all that stuff.

Then I spent some time
reading seniors' autobiographies
in a class I had invented
when the department chairman
said "Hey, we got these books
so use 'em."

I read
about first love and lost love
and moving and changing
and growing and longing
and laughing and hurting.

I read things
that amused me and confused me
and sobered me and bored me
and delighted me and scared me
and angered me,

and I read about
her Mom's suicide and his dog dying
and his alcoholic mother and her parents' divorce
and his Dad's death in Viet Nam
and her little sister's leukemia,

and I knew that there was more to this than
ten years of teaching
adjectives and verbs
and to not write run on sentences.

The Museum of Teaching

There are museums for almost everything:
history, science, baseball, automobiles,
music, art, you name it.
And these are just the big ones.

Why, in NY alone, we have museums to
bottles, maple trees, kazoos, Jell-o, gloves,
salt, carrousels, whales, guitars, farms and,
well, you get the picture.

So naturally enough I would assume
there would be a museum of teaching,
a place where all the accomplishments of
this noble profession would be enshrined,
displayed for all to see and admire.

I had never actually seen one, you understand,
but having a pretty good sense for this sort of thing,
I headed for the nearest bookstore
and did some serious browsing.

So I located museums for cement, beer cans,
dog mushing, oysters and even
The 24 hour Church of Elvis and Museum
in Portland Oregon, over the Thai restaurant

The index of the Book of Little Museums
skipped from *Tattoo Art* to *Teddy Bears*,

no listing of *Teaching*, no museum as tribute
to the ages-old role of teachers.

Back on the street, I hailed a cab —
cabbies have all the answers, I reasoned.
"Where to Mac?" as we left the curb.
"Is there a teacher museum in this town?"
"Teacher museum? This town?"

The cab swung back to the curb.
"Buddy, you don't need a cab.
Just get out…look around.
You're already there…the teachers museum is the whole world."

RANDOM THOUGHTS:

Waiting

Seventh grade boys who
weigh about seventy pounds
fear the girls who are

bigger and stronger,
waiting for the day when they
will be able to

talk without fear of
sounding like an old hinge
and be tall enough

to see
and be seen
in the hall.

Introspection

Every now and then
I find myself irritated
at a student
for behaving the way that I did
in eighth grade

and I hope that I respond
as well as my teachers did.

Autobiography

She didn't really want
to write her autobiography—
only the part that

She really didn't
want to remember but was
all she ever could

She hasn't got much
to say that anybody
would want to read.

Who cares about what
happened to her when she was six
and seven and eight

and until she and Mom
moved to this town, away
from good old uncle Bob?

A Buck Seventy-eight

So I get this letter
from a father whose son is a
product of maternal
indulgence and apologizing
suggesting that maybe I don't know
my ass from my elbow
about teaching
and wants to know
why I'm more interested in grabbing
the big tax dollars he pays
than I am about teaching.

So after I explain that
he came to his conclusion without
being armed with all the facts of the matter
and he turns red
and apologizes several times
and winds up explaining
through teary eyes
what things are like at home
and apologizes a few more times
and tells me to go ahead
and give his son another detention
and he'll be sure it gets served.

I decide I won't embarrass him
by returning the buck seventy-eight
I have in my pocket,
which I figure is his share of my salary
and I walk out of the room
feeling lousy
for planning to in the first place,
knowing full well that tomorrow the kid
will bring in another excuse from mom.

An Odd Kid

In eighth grade,
Johnny liked to talk about plants,
what he grew and why.
A loner, an odd kid.

He was still into it in high school,
growing things,
plants he couldn't even get high on.
A loner, an odd kid.

A few years later, I saw him in a market,
just up from Florida,
with some race horses he was training.
Sleeping in the horse barn,
a loner, an odd kid.

Two years ago,
dead of AIDS,
he rated a news article, not just an obituary,
public testimony to his life as
a loner, an odd kid.

Teachers recalled him as that.
"Really into plants, flowers and stuff," they said.
"Trained horses," I added.
"A loner, an odd kid," they affirmed.

He loved living things
plants, animals, people.
Too bad that's what makes
a loner, an odd kid.

First Person Singular

At my school
with a minority population of
less than two percent,
diversity has to do with differences
in height
or hair color
or who you hang out with.

To the lone African American
student in my class
I tried to explain
the correctness of
"I am"
versus the incorrectness of
"I be."

I am? You mean like
I am black?
I am different?
I am teased?
I am bullied?
I am afraid?
I am alone?

Hey—why not just let me be?

(Paraphrasing Chicago's song, *25 or 6 to 4*)

25 or 6 Two More

I had done this for 25 years, maybe 26,
depending on the Retirement System's records.
With bonus time included
I could possibly retire in two years.

Plus, I was getting close to my 3000th student
which would round things off nicely,
and I believe we are allowed, even encouraged
to retire at 3000.

And that would be a nice round number—3000

So as # 3000 left my room on the last day of that year,
I would ask him or her to drop my keys off in the office,
and I would ride off into the sunset, so to speak.

But—what if #3001 needed me?

To Some Retiring Friends

Years pass, unnoticed, uncounted
Students too; hundreds, thousands
many now nameless, faceless
to you, but not the other way.

You may not know them now,
but they know you.

You took them somewhere
unreachable without you.

You gave them
what they needed,
(perhaps more).

They remember
what you've done—

counseled
disciplined
tested

prodded
coached
driven
encouraged

We remember
what you've done—

Given of yourselves
for them,
for us.

Thank you.

To My Teacher

Sometimes I am lost.
Take my hand—lead me.

Help me understand
what you are teaching

I know it is more than
it seems—more than
just the definition of
plot or what makes irony

I know it is important
or you would not know it.
You would not teach it.
You would not want so
much for it to
be part of me.

But I am lost sometimes.
What makes things important?

What makes them worth knowing?
Why am I worth teaching it to?
What will I do with it?
What makes me worth your time,
your effort
your pain?
Am I that special to you?

Sometimes I am lost.
Take my hand—lead me.

Keep it Simple

First day of school
for both my granddaughter
and me.

Kate's first,
my twenty-first

I always make it
something tricky—
the first step of a quest
to make something meaningful
of 125 eighth graders—
a great responsibility—
a magnificent Holy Grail-like search for
some great truth—
some essential knowledge.

She, on the other hand,
made some friends
and had a snack.

Wm. C. Jr.

William was a pain in the butt.

I tried my best to make allowances for
his father being in jail
his being in a foster home
his being a city kid in a country school and
his having the social skills of a hyena

But it wasn't good enough and when
he got suspended
I was happy and when
he got sent to the Alternative Ed. program
I was really happy.

And I know there wasn't anything
I could have done to change things

but when the handwritten addendum
to the attendance list told me that
Wm. C. Jr. left as of 10/23
I was angry at myself.

Guru

I've always wanted to be a guru,
my disciples gathered around me
entreating me to provide them
with some great truth
some key to their existence,
a word which would propel them to greatness.
"Master, what is the meaning of life?"
for example.

My students on the other hand

seem to seek lesser truths,
keys to somewhat less lofty ambition
yet, desiring the answers to questions
as seemingly unanswerable
as the meaning of life.
"How long should it be?"
"Does spelling count?"

It's neither that I can't answer those questions
nor that I don't want to
but they hardly seem worthy of a guru.

on the other hand,
I don't know the meaning of life
and if I did I sure wouldn't be here
teaching English and I
don't think I would get much of a kick out
sitting in a lotus position all day
dispensing esoteric advice anyway.

Let's just leave it that the piece should be
long enough to get the job done,
and of course spelling counts.

Living in Another Land

She sat in the back of the room—
Just across the border that separates
The land of the regular kids
From the uncharted territory she calls home.

It's a beautifully vibrant land—
Rolling, fruitful plains of imagination and creativity,
Vast, deep oceans of talent and potential
Majestic mountains of eccentric, quirky behavior.

It's also a somber land—
A great desert of loneliness,
Uncrossable chasms of isolation,
Manmade barriers of stereotyped expectation.

I didn't visit her often enough—
The border crossing was arduous,
And I would have to leave too much
At the customs house.

Nobody Told Me

In teacher school,
they failed to tell me
about certain things I would need to know,
like hugging the mother of a student,
a mother, a stranger, who clung to me
near his casket,
with grief's old-friend-tightness,
and whispered in my ear
what a good boy he was,
and how proud they were of him,
and how they hoped
he would have been in my class next year,
and that I would have enjoyed
having him as a student.

And they didn't tell me about
looking into the eyes of students
who were his friends and
seeing the confusion,
and the pain they felt
at a turn of events that didn't fit
how they thought life
should be.

Rhetorical

I used to be taken aback a bit
when a conversation began
with someone saying to me:
"I thought you had retired –
How much longer before you do?"

It used to bother me,
but I have mellowed.
Now it only bothers me if it's said
By an administrator
after my observation.

Between the Lines

All that prevents him from
devoting his total attention
to the baseball game
is the pile of student writing
between him and the TV,
a stack of cliches and
tired metaphors
worn out by a thousand previous users
and abusers
of the language.

He sifts through the pile
looking for one which will
motivate him to continue on
to a second and a third,
and so forth,
a metaphorical rounding of the bases,
until he has reduced the pile to nothing,
and able to turn his full attention to
the Yankees and Red Sox.

Glancing above his glasses to catch the replay
of Derek Jeter rocking a line drive
off the green monster
and only getting a single
he ponders the mysterious twist of baseball fate
that penalizes a player for hitting the ball
too hard
like he is penalizing himself for caring
too much
about grading these papers.

Writing My Own Epitaph

Who among us would dare write the words
that would identify us for all time as
"English Teacher?"

Not I, thank you.
I haven't the courage to risk eternity
lying (or is it laying?) beneath a stone
on which has been carved
my misspelling
or grammar/usage error
or apostrophe incorrectly inserted or omitted
or another error so egregious that
below the words
"Here lies an English teacher"
someone might scrawl
"But not a very good one, it seems."

A Haiku for When Open House Occurs Three Weeks into the School Year

A parent asks me
"How's Bobby doing so far?"
(Which one is Bobby?)

Help from Yogi

Sound planning makes up
ninety percent of teaching
What's the other half?

A Pretty Good Way

I have a pretty good way with students
who have ability,
but are determined to not do a lick of work.

I take them into the hall,
so as to not embarrass them,
while the class wonders what's going on,
waiting to hear my voice
rise as it sometimes does,
to the point of having other teachers thank me
for quieting down their classes
in the eighth grade hall.

So, I engage my sincere voice,
but also my coach's voice,
and my drill sergeant's voice,
and talk to him about how
it's really a shame for him
to do so well in class discussion,

and then show up,
day after day,
with no work done.

And he smiles and swears he will do better,
because he knows he can, and wants to,
and I check his homework the next day
and write another zero next to his name.

Pretty Good Way, Redux

And the next year,
I have the same conversation
with his brother.

Triumph

It has been said that Julius Caesar,
returning to Rome from a campaign,
honored with a *triumph,*
the great parade down the Via Appia
accorded victorious Roman generals,
would ride in his chariot with a slave behind him,
who whispered in Caesar's ear,
This too shall pass,
to remind him of the fragile and tenuous nature of victory.

If I were to have such a procession,
returning from a classic victory
on behalf of the English language,
I would replace the slave with an eighth grader,
whispering in my ear:

I don't know. Like, um, it was a really OK win and stuff,
but, um, it wouldn't be, um, like something that would be

like around all the time and stuff. Or maybe it would or something. Whatever.

Perception is Reality

I may have become what I always
thought English teachers were—
people who hang out in bookstores
and leaf through books,
and write poetry, like I am doing now.

Of course, I never suspected they
might do these things because
they actually enjoyed them, but because
it was a requirement—the result of a
pledge they must make when they become teachers,
a swearing in,
a profession of allegiance to the written word,
while at the same time
promising to avoid all other forms of
relatively normal behavior.

I always assumed that in warmer weather
male English teachers must wear Bermuda shorts
with wing tips and black silk socks.

I pictured them rolling up their sleeves and
tucking their neckties between
the second and third buttons,
as they fired up the hibachi on a Saturday afternoon.

Writers cramp would be their injury of choice,
and the stories they told in the faculty lounge
would relate to
how many dangling participles they

had circled in red that week.

So when I run into my students in Borders,
they don't see my copy of *Poets and Writers*
hidden inside *The Sporting News*.

Progress

I used to just show up,
teach,
go home.

Then somebody told me
I needed a better lesson plan.

I had to define my standards and objectives,
gather materials,
establish an anticipatory set,
determine the duration of the lesson.

Then I needed to give my input,
model,
check for understanding,
question, using appropriate strategies,
conduct guided practice,
attain closure,
assign independent practice.
Then I could go home.

Resurrection

Teaching is about
recreating ourselves,
changing, evolving,
surrendering annually

to the heat of late June,
consumed by our own fire,
burning ourselves to ash –
the residue of our own intensity.

And in September,
rising, Phoenix-like,
with new life, new energy,
to fly on strong
new wings.

Equalizer

I met a woman in a book store
who said that she had heard good things about me
in the education community—
and that she was signed up for a couple of my workshops
and couldn't wait to take them.

My ego was bathed in a warm glow.
I smiled and took on a knowing sort of air—
perhaps nodding a bit and being charming
in an intellectual sort of way.

Then I sat back down to grade the papers
that I had brought with me and
discovered that I was not such a big deal as
either of us thought.

SECTION THREE

THE WONDERFUL WORLD OF METAPHYSICS
THE NEW AGE MOVEMENT: *not so new*
THE SOUND OF SILENCE: *the comfort of meditation*
THE HIGHER SELF: *get acquainted with the real you*
CONNECTING WITH YOUR POWER OF COURAGE
A BIT ABOUT CHAKRAS: *why the new kids
need to know about them*
REIKI: *how it relates to the new kids*

The Voice

Listen for the voice.
It will speak loudly,
Softly,
urgently,
calmly.

It will be assertive.
It will be frightened.
It will be proud.
It will be plaintive.

It will scream.
It will beg.
It will laugh.
It will cry.

It will speak in odd places,
odd styles,
odd words.

It will tell you things you need to know,
it will tell you things you don't.

It will tell you things you want to know,
it will tell you things you won't.

And when it does,
Listen.

INTRODUCTION TO METAPHYSICS:
Beyond the Five Senses

Most of us accept that the five senses we learned about in elementary school are all we have to perceive with. We learned about the sense of seeing, hearing, touch, taste and smell.

We use our eyes to read and recognize familiar faces, our ears to take in voices and music and the myriad of sounds around us. Our hands and other parts of our body give and receive touch. Our sense of taste allows us to savor the last piece of chocolate in the box or to spit out the mashed peas we were asked to swallow as an infant. To smell the first flowers of spring brings joy and anticipation of basking in the warmth of summer.

What we fail to realize is that while these five senses serve to identify some of the physical elements that makes us human; waiting to be discovered is the ultimate gift given to the human being; the spiritual self.

In the next few chapters we will explore senses that are considered to be metaphysical, meaning beyond the physical.

Some of you may be very knowledgeable about metaphysical principles and practices and have integrated them into your lives. Some know the term and a little bit about it, while some are standing on the outskirts, a little apprehensive about stepping into the realm of the unseen world.

In reading the following chapters, you may find a statement or even a single word that intrigues you or prompts you to continue and explore your perceptions and beliefs. Perhaps something will awaken that long-forgotten curiosity that you have tucked away, maybe since childhood. It is a safe place to examine your thoughts, fears and feelings about the metaphysical world. So, please read, discover, question, ponder, be skeptical, or even reject the information.

To question, is to begin to understand. Author unknown

To those who fully embrace metaphysical principles, please consider how important these approaches are to educating the new kids.

Dolores R. Card, Hermon R. Card

The Incoming Soul

A new soul makes its entrance into life and its earthly journey begins. Within this new soul is the potential for his/her life. This perfect child brings with it all gifts, talents, human qualities, and abilities needed to complete its purpose on Earth. There is one constant that we must learn to believe. This new person is perfect and the blueprint for this perfection can never be altered or eliminated, no matter what life brings. Within our inner self, *we are forever perfect.*

What happens during the life span of this newborn will be determined by a variety of factors, including karma, challenges, choices made, family values and situations beyond his/her control, which are often due to choices made by others. One of the major factors for a successful life comes through the education process.

How we determine and instruct what is important to the physical, intellectual, emotional and spiritual aspects of this new individual is how we increase and empower, or diminish, his/her potential.

This complex human being is a clean slate and needs to be guided and nourished. In these early years, they do not have many choices as to what we present to them and attitudes and beliefs begin to form. We need to acknowledge that how we judge the world is based on our beliefs. Even the very young, especially the new kids, know instinctively what they need and begin to react when they perceive they are being coerced or forced into accepting the beliefs of others.

Mostly we miss those signals and chalk it up to being "fussy" or behaving badly. In truth, they are displaying the beginning of many years of frustration of not being understood. Very often they are admonished, which can shut down their attempts of self-discovery.

Effective education directs its efforts to reach and encourage a child's natural instincts to learn and to help them to develop a positive attitude, to activate their inner belief system. There is a whole world coming into their awareness and they need to investigate by using all of their senses, known and unknown. They need to feel safe to come forward with their thoughts and feelings about the direction they want their life to take. They need the freedom to interpret their own lives. We all need that freedom.

Those born into the current generation are highly intuitive and require that whatever education system they are in allows them to not only cultivate, but to be able to use this ability to augment the learning process.

CHAPTER SEVEN

We shall require a substantially new way of thinking if mankind is to survive.
Albert Einstein

THE WONDERFUL WORLD OF METAPHYSICS:
Don't be afraid, you can come in, it isn't scary, and it relates to our current students.

Origins and Nature of Metaphysics

Metaphysics is a branch of philosophy concerned with explaining and clarifying the fundamental notions by which people understand the world, e.g., existence, objects and their properties, space and time, cause and effect and possibility. It is also the study of all phenomena within the universe. Prior to the modern history of science, scientific questions were addressed as part of metaphysics known as natural philosophy.

A person who studies metaphysics is known as a metaphysicist or a metaphysician.

The new kid, Aristotle highly valued its study and referred to metaphysics as "the first philosophy." Its issues were considered no less important than the other main formal subjects of physical science, medicine, mathematics, poetics and music.

Aristotle's *Metaphysics* was divided into three parts, which are now regarded as the proper branches of traditional metaphysics:

- **Ontology:** The study of being and existence; includes the definition and classification of individual physical or mental, the nature of their properties, the nature of change.

- **Natural Theology:** The study of God or Gods; involves many topics, including among others the nature of religion and the world, existence of the divine, questions about creation, and the numerous religious or spiritual issues that concern humankind in general.

- **Universal Science:** The study of first principles, such as the *law of noncontradiction*, which Aristotle believed were the foundation of all other inquiries

Although metaphysics goes back to Aristotelian philosophy, Aristotle himself credited earlier philosophers with dealing with metaphysical questions. It was considered the "queen of sciences" even before the age of Aristotle. Scientific questions in ancient Greece were referred to metaphysicians. Latin Scholars referred to metaphysics as "the science beyond the physical. "

Socrates and Plato although supportive of metaphysical principles, were in contrast to Aristotle, who professed a more inclusive form of philosophy instead of an existence in isolation. This way of thinking survived well into the 1100-1500s. The scope of philosophy was linked to the technique of deducing the nature of the world by pure reason.

A school of metaphysics was founded in fifth century Italy and its teaching was centered on the supposition that logical standards of clarity were the criteria for truth. As with other disciplines and theories introduced through the ages, there have always been detractors, dependant on who is doing the assessing of the theories.

In the 18th century a number of individuals suggested that much of metaphysics should be rejected, arguing that all genuine knowledge involves either mathematics or matters of fact that can be empirically proven. Suffice it to say that this premise leaves no room for critical thinking.

Early in the 20th century, even though science was making great advances, there was a sharp decline in support of metaphysics. In the second half of the century however, subjects of metaphysical research were found to be entirely physical and natural, thus making them part of science proper.

Quantum physics has been gaining similar recognition from a purely scientific perspective. The two systems are growing so close in nature that the term metaphysical and quantum physics are becoming widely viewed as synonymous. It can be said that science is finally catching up to what our enlightened ancestors have know all along. It is now that we can realize that science and spirituality are turning the next page together.

The Value of Metaphysics

There is a purely practical component to metaphysics. Scientists, including Immanual Kant, Alexandre Koyre, David Hull and, of course, the renowned new kid, Albert Einstein, published books declaring the role of metaphysics in scientific theorizing. It supplied an even deeper component to the "why factor".

Kant, in his *Critique of Pure Reason*, argued for the freedom of the will and the existence of "things in themselves", and that facts may be attainable independent of experience.[1]

Koyre declared in his book, *Metaphysics and Measurement*, "It is not by following experiment, but by outstripping experiment, that the scientific mind makes progress." [2]

Biologist, David Hull has argued that changes in the ontological status of humans as they evolved spiritually have been central in the development of biological thought. He went on to say that Darwin's ignorance of metaphysics made it more difficult to respond to his critics because he could not readily grasp the ways in which their underlying metaphysical views differed from his own.[3]

In physics, new metaphysical ideas have arisen in connection to quantum mechanics, leading physicists like Einstein to propose alternative theories than retained determinism, which is a theory that a precise combination of events at a particular time engenders a particular outcome. This does not leave much room for variables.

Despite positions of skepticism and concerns of validity, the phenomenon of occurrences beyond our understanding and ability to define, remain part of our unseen reality and inner acknowledgement of possibilities.

Centuries of mystical experiences by humans, although considered abstract and not verifiable are not any different than our acceptance of other abstract concepts such as love or freedom. What becomes commonplace, many times, is accepted as truth.

Metaphysics and the Current Students

The dictionary defines metaphysics from two root words: "meta" (beyond) and "physics" (of material substance). It literally means "what lies beyond our physical world, beyond the physical senses." The human five senses, touch, taste, sound, smell and sight, are extremely limited. If we are left with just our five senses to interpret the reality of our world, we would be wrong about almost everything.

Our current students live by this viewpoint and are trying to bring into focus the reality that is beyond what is perceptible to the physical senses. They understand that there are both empirical and conceptual aspects of reason. They not only can draw a distinction between the two, but function well in interpreting both physical and abstract propositions. To, in any way, hamper the development of this innate skill, is to not only deter their efforts, but can lead to an apathetic attitude of "why bother?"

Styles and Methods of Metaphysics

Rational vs. Empirical. Rationalism is a method or a theory "in which the criterion of the truth is not sensory", but intellectual and deductive. Rationalist metaphysicians aim to deduce the nature of reality by priori reasoning. Empiricism holds that the senses are primary source of knowledge about the world.

Analytical vs. Systemic. The systems building style of metaphysics attempts to answer all the important questions in a comprehensive and coherent way, providing a theory of everything or complete picture of the world. The contrasting approach is to deal with problems gradually, in increments.

Dogmatic vs. Critical. Under the scholastic approach of the Middle Ages, a number of themes and ideas were not open to be challenged. Kant and others thought this dogmatism should be replaced by a critical approach.

Individual vs. Collective. Scholasticism and Analytical philosophy are examples of collaborative approaches to philosophy. Many other philosophers expounded individual visions.

Descriptive vs. Revisionary. Descriptive metaphysics sets out to investigate our deepest assumptions and revisionary metaphysics sets out to improve or rectify them.

Today's students attempt to find unity between experience and thought. They are concerned with developing their intellectual potential as well as exploring the personal meaning of their lives. The new kids have the ability to utilize all forms of assessment, but their education requires bringing latent ideas to their consciousness to discover and expand their competence. Curricular emphasis needs to use methods to help students discover and clarify knowledge as well as exercise critical thinking.

Rather than passing down organized bodies of knowledge to new learners, teach students to apply their own knowledge through experimenting with their innate abilities and style of learning. They must be allowed to incorporate their inherent capabilities that are now considered outside the realm of established educational tenets.

While probably not referring to the new kids, or the missing piece of our current education system, the following quote from Einstein seems to address both: *The intuitive mind is a sacred gift and the rational mind is a faithful servant. We have created a society that honors the servant and has forgotten the gift.*

Schools need to be practical in preparing students to become valuable members of society, and at the same time, be open to assisting and strengthening them to become a driving force for positive change. If the cultivation of the intellect is the highest priority in a worthwhile education, the essential piece is to allow that intellect to be utilized according to the capacity of the student.

By allowing students to employ all of their distinctive means to examine information they become responsible for their conclusions and decisions which can broaden character development. This kind of education will not think of students as objects to be measured, tracked or standardized. Such methods would provide opportunities for self-direction and self-awareness, which must start with the student and not the curriculum content.

Students need to be allowed to develop their intuition as part of learning. New kids need to be able to find their passion for learning as a means of discovery and be taught to feel their strength.

We need to create an education system where books are tools, rather than the authority. Basic changes in human nature, seen through observation and recorded through documentation, show that our consciousness is changing and advancing rapidly. *Students have changed, our education system has not.*

CHAPTER EIGHT

*We have entered into a new phase of evolution...
we have developed language to exchange information,
producing us, but we are more than our genes.*
Stephen Hawking

NEW AGE MOVEMENT:
not so new

New Age History

What we refer to as the New Age Movement is hardly new. Its philosophy is rooted in ancient traditions and has existed in various forms since the 2nd century. Even as recently as 1804, William Blake referred to it in his poem, *Rouse Up, O Young Men of the New Age.*[1]

There have always been men and women within primitive societies who were looked upon as possessing special knowledge and power. Medicine men or shamans were called upon to maintain contact with the spiritual world for a specific clan. This is still a practice among many societies today.

When communities became more complex and organized, societies began to form groups or guilds to ensure the continuation of these practices.

Covert traditions were handed down to the next generation in early spiritual groups, communes and fraternities. These groups needed to be cautious lest they be accused of heresy. Yet, in spite of all hindrances and opposition, spiritual traditions began to reach far and wide.

There were, however, periods of decline and revival of spiritual practices, often as a result of cultural and political conditions. In Europe, for example, interest in ancient spiritual traditions was revived at various times.

From the 7th to the 5th century BCE, Greek and other philosophers, including Confucius, attempted to transcend the old myths and superstitions of their time and present a more in-depth approach to the spiritual nature of humans. An abstract mystical way of seeing and experiencing reality was coming to light.

In later centuries, arcane doctrines in Christianity, Gnosticism and Jewish mysticism (Kabbala) contributed to and influenced our understanding of puzzling and often confusing principles. Some of these sensitive traditions became embodied in Greek culture and made their way into the Western world.

The Age of Enlightenment; our current age? Not really. Even though it sounds current, it began about 1687 with the publication of Isaac Newton's *Mathematical Principles of Natural Philosophy*,[2] the basis of exploring nature in an objective manner. Newton, a British scientist, and another most important new kid, ushered in the Scientific Revolution, which evolved into the Age of Reason, the direct influence of our present New Age Movement. The Scientific Revolution brought to an end the medieval view and replaced it with our modern understanding of physics, nature, biology and human beings. The idea of freedom of thought emerged and provided strong support for mystical practices by lessening the fear of theological information.

Later in the 1700s a greater respect for Eastern philosophy emerged and spiritual traditions grew. The spiritual movement gained a new following.

Andrew Jackson Davis became one of the founders of modern spiritualism in the United States. Spiritualism gained additional momentum in 1848 in Hydesville, New York, when the Fox family claimed to communicate with a deceased man. It became nationwide news and led to the practice of what we now call channeling. Even President Abraham Lincoln had contact with mediums and took part in séances.

Lily Dale, a spiritualist community, was established in southwestern New York State around 1880. Word of this unique community spread and soon became a place of pilgrimage for spiritualists throughout the world. It became known as the home of spiritualism in the United States. It is still visited by thousands of people each year. Typical guest lecturers include: John Edwards, Dr. Wayne Dyer and Deepak Chopra.

In Europe the spiritualist movement was well under way by the 19th century with millions of believers, finding its way into mainstream thinking. It was Madame H.P. Blavatsky who forged the European arcane tradition by founding the Theosophical Society in 1875, which is still part of the foundation of the Modern New Age Movement. Other pioneers in the field of metaphysics include C.W. Leadbeater and Alice Bailey. They all proposed that there was and would continue to be stages of human development that would facilitate spiritual growth and evolutionary changes to adjust to each global period. Madame Blavatsky offered a new vision of the concept of life in the universe, which was opposite of the narrow-minded dogmatic outlook of the time. She introduced the concept of reincarnation and karma, now household words.

Current New Age: a renaissance of sorts

The fastest growth of New Age practices has been in the United States. Our forefathers, including Benjamin Franklin, George Washington and John Adams, as well as noted authors Henry David Thoreau and Ralph Waldo Emerson were influenced by spiritualistic thought. The reverse side of the Great Seal of the United States reads: A new order of the Age begins.

New Age concepts, doctrines and principles have been brought forth through a variety of groups in the 20th century including the Rosicrucians, Free Masonry and the teachings of Edgar Cayce, known as The Sleeping Prophet.

The renewed interest in spiritual traditions has had a tremendous impact on the minds of the two most recent generations. The most contemporary revival of New Age philosophy was primarily a movement among the younger generation in the late sixties that demanded to play a greater part in all aspects of society. It was one of the greatest decades for new kids to foster social changes. Originally called the Age of Aquarius to signify the new era of spiritual endorsement as foretold in Astrology, in the early 70s the name New Age was adopted.

This New Age is far from over. It grew in popularity in the '70s and '80s. Entering the 21st century, it has reached a state of maturity despite the broad spectrum from commercialization to the unselfish dedication to serving humankind. It is exemplified by harmony and enlightenment, accompanied by social and personal transformation, a greater emergence of holistic medicine and a significant growth of spiritual awareness.

New Age groups are often distinguished by their practice of psychic readings, Tarot cards, yoga, meditation and the study of astrology. They also believe in various natural healing practices as a partner with traditional medicine, including: acupuncture, herbal therapy, natural foods and utilizing the body's natural healing systems through the practice of Reiki and other energy techniques.

The common goal of the 21st century New Age advocate is the eradication of hunger, sickness, poverty, racism, sexism and war. The new kids are solidly immersed in all of these causes as well as the restructuring of social and political systems that no longer work for the highest interest of the people on this planet.

We, as a species, have shifted and changed through our time on Earth and our history directly relates to the students in our current classrooms. Each advance in awareness are all hallmarks of spiritual growth, guiding the way to oneness, sharing and collaboration, leading to changing the way we communicate, socialize and form alliances to create a better world. These measures enable people to express themselves in creative ways, stay in touch with love ones and unify for both individual and global causes.

As humanity passed through each of its periods, each age was marked by distinctive characteristics and achievements. Although we don't necessarily know the individual names, I'm sure there were catalysts for change during Earth's early years. Perhaps the aforementioned Lucy of Ethiopia was one of those early pioneers.

Why then, is it not realistic to believe that a "new kind" of human being is needed to use the technology and advanced ideas and theories of this current age. How often do we say about a child, something like, "He is exactly like his grandpa John." Is he? There may be a striking physical resemblance or even tendencies for speech patterns or gestures, but there will also be the differences that will allow that child to adapt to the world he will grow up in, reacting to all the environmental, social and internal influences on his life.

If we accept as truth the scientific evidence of our evolution through the ages, why would we hinder or even deny the needs of this new generation and the tools needed to be those catalysts who have come to change society, bringing new inventions, discovering cures for diseases and helping the people of this planet work together to bring peace in this age.

However you view this information, whether scientific, astrological, metaphysical or plain theoretical, we cannot ignore or dismiss the exceptional and distinctive traits of the most recent residents of this planet, who have been among us for at least the last 30 years. Whatever label or name you lend to this phenomenon, the irrefutable evidence is that as humans shifted into different ages, they also shifted in consciousness in order to meet the needs of the incoming age.

It is not a coincidence that they are here, at this time, bringing with them their quirkiness and unique ways of looking at the world. They need to be able to utilize their abilities. They are trying to bring new patterns of both energy and intention. A major way to ensure this shift is an education system that allows the freedom to explore what they already know how to do.

The Ages Through Astrology

The metaphysicians of the ancient world had a profound understanding of the principles of evolution according to astrology. They recognized all life as being in stages of becoming human in consciousness as well as in intellect. The proficiency of those who studied the planets and constellations without the benefit of telescopes in ancient time is astounding. Astronomical observatories have been discovered in all parts of the world.

Our ancestors were much closer to nature than we are today; they had a greater connection to how what happened in the cosmos affected life on Earth. It appears to those that study astrology, that ages coincide with the movement of the Earth around the sun. The sun remains in each house (astrological sign) for approximately 2,160 years, which is considered an astrological age.

Astrological literature has informed us about the qualities and attributes of those born under each of the astrological signs or houses. How many times have you read about the sign you were born under and marveled, "That is exactly how I am!" or who hasn't turned to the horoscope page in the newspaper to have a quick look at your horoscope for the day and mostly dismiss it as folly. But, at the same time, there is a slight trace of a remaining thought that says, "hmmmmm?"

Our Current Ages: their traits and qualities

We are entering into a period of apex, which will lead to events that will alter life as we know it; the ending of a 2000 plus year civilization and the beginning of creating a new one. We are preparing to establish new modes of social living and relationships based on cooperation and sharing. There is a prevailing awareness that we are standing at the beginning of a new era, a new cosmic cycle. We are facing a crisis, which is essentially spiritual, but is working out in the political and economic fields, as well as how we educate.

In order to better understand the age we are entering, we need to go back to look at the traits and qualities of the previous one, the Piscean Age. The cycle of ages does not begin and end on a given day, but gradually advance into the next. We are, at this point, feeling the effects of both.

Symbolized by the fish, Pisceans act as one, each being a part of the greater whole. Have you ever seen a school of fish? They act as one. As Pisceans are spiritual in nature and tend to express themselves emotionally, their beliefs enter into both their strengths and weaknesses. Extremely compassionate for those in need, which is their greatest strength, can also suppress their capability to set personal boundaries. Confusion is the Piscean's potential weakness, often putting them at a disadvantage to find clarity of purpose.

Pisces represents sacrifice, charity, mercy, compassion and forgiveness. This sign is also associated with sacred sites and sanctuaries. During the 2,160 years of the Piscean Age, Christianity developed and countless religious conflicts and crusades were carried out, most notably in the middle ages.

It was also the age of re-vitalization, as distinguished by the Renaissance and later centuries saw great leaps in medicine and inventions to benefit humankind. Overall an age of tremendous progress, both internally and externally. Because Venus was a great authority in Pisces, the message of love was fundamental in this era.

The Age of Aquarius

Following the logic of astrology, we are entering into the Age of Aquarius. While the emphasis for the Piscean Age was individual progress, the Age of Aquarius focuses its energies toward oneness and global connection. Technically, it will be two or three hundred years before we will experience the Age of Aquarius to its maximum. Until then we will feel its effects increasing in increments.

The Attributes and Characteristics of the Aquarian Age

- The outstanding quality is synthesis, the blending and fusing of the presently divided humanity into a whole.
- A new sense of oneness with all creation will replace the present sense of separation.
- The present fear and confusion will give way to a new freedom and sense of meaning and purpose to life.
- Cooperation will replace competition and tolerance and compassion will replace greed and hate.
- Major developments in science, many medical breakthroughs to cure diseases, new ways to educate.
- To break free of centuries of false doctrines and the destruction of resources, and the commitment of the healing of the physical Earth.
- There will be a new perspective about love. Love will have nothing to do with possession or ego. The idea of "you belong to me" ends with this new age.
- It is an age characterized by technical progress, by technology, spectacular inventions, media, medications, Internet, super information devises, computers, smart cards, smart phones and more to come.

We are already witnessing some of the signs of the Aquarian Age. We have sent an astronaut to the moon. There are no longer any frontiers on Earth and in some ways we have transcended the limits of space and time. We are already a society based on knowledge, information and communication. We must refocus our efforts in the pursuit of excellence and mutual respect. We can still draw from the qualities of the Piscean Age to show love compassion and generosity toward our companions on this earthly journey. We must find a way to provide an educational environment for our young to be able to discover and cultivate their own moral code.

It is appropriate to ask why we were born and what our mission on Earth is. The Age of Aquarius invites us to show altruism and favor scientific, systematic or technological solutions and at the same time, find a balance with our spiritual character. If we look at how the ages and their qualities change as needed, we can clearly see how life on Earth changed as we moved through them.

The very beginnings of the Aquarian Age began during the time of the French Revolution. The popular slogan was *freedom, equality, fraternity*, three values that still motivate our progression as a species.

In short, these two ages offer us the opportunity to broaden our divine character by showing love for the self and others. The motto of the Piscean Age was: *I believe*. The motto of the Age of Aquarius is: *I know*. We are being asked to discover the best parts of humanity and raise them to a higher plane, bringing us to a new way of understanding our existence.

We are in the process of creating new patterns that hold the key to solving our energy crisis, global warming, disease, hunger, homelessness, war and every other human miscreation. We need to attain our financial freedom, reverse our poverty consciousness and no longer accept that we are damaged and limited.

There is an intense cleansing and purging taking place on this planet and yes, in the outer world it looks like we are heading for a global economic collapse as our financial systems are being turned upside down. Individuals and systems that are taking part in unethical and even unlawful behavior will be brought to light. It is an arduous, complex, and at times, painful process, but if we are to make revisions that will discover and eradicate the abuse of power, we need to validate those that will bring us through this crisis.

Our students, that we call the new kids, are trying to do just that. They are trying to bring the current chaos to a new order. They are listening to their inner promptings. They are trying to find the balance between their inner self and the comprehension of their potential to use their new energy to open the door into the Age of Aquarius.

What doesn't matter is whether you believe in reincarnation or karma or any of the aspects of New Age thinking. What does matter is that you believe that there is an essential quality in our young people that is not being recognized in our current education system and that we need to address that aspect—**now.**

CHAPTER NINE

Quiet the mind and the soul will speak.
Majaya Sati Bhagavat

THE SOUND OF SILENCE:
the comfort and power of meditation

Meditation, to some, seems out of reach because of the emphasis made on the time it takes, the implied rigid rules of the procedures and lack of belief in their ability to quiet their mind. Many know that it carries great benefits, including improving health, but as our lives become busier, meditation is not high on the list of priorities. The irony is that it is the practice of meditation that can lessen the stress of our multi-tasking lives.

How we think about meditation is critical to being able to achieve a meditative state. Perhaps it would help to gain a perspective on what meditation is and how it works.

Very few of us have the opportunity, much less the time it takes, to sit on a mountain top in a lotus position for days, weeks or even months. That certainly would be a profound experience, but not necessary for the average person to do to reap the benefits of meditation.

Many everyday acts that we carry out amount to meditation. When we daydream, we shift into a soft focus, many times blocking out what is going on around us. If we deliberate on a single issue, for instance, deeply thinking over a decision or finding a solution to a problem, our attention is narrowed to the issue at hand. Don't ever be afraid to just sit and think. *Concentrated thought, no matter what the subject, becomes meditation.*

The Role of the Brain

The most essential knowledge to understanding meditation is the function of the human brain as it applies to our spiritual nature. There is much more to learn about how the brain works and there is extensive research being conducted that will promote our collective understanding of the workings of the mind in order to enter into a deeper state of self awareness.

We know that we use our brain to solve puzzles, to plan our daily lives, plus numerous other tasks. The brain wants to be in charge and will continue to repeat the patterns we have programmed into it unless we take charge and change those patterns. The brain is constantly filtering out hundreds of pieces of information, storing data and telling you how to feel and act. Meditation is a process of taming the mind to work in partnership with us.

Because our brain doesn't know the difference between a memory and an image we are creating internally at the moment, meditation can "trick" our brain into cooperating with what we are asking it to do.

Altered States

The attainment of a meditative state happens in many ways, whether by conscious effort or not, but is always contingent upon being in an altered state.

An altered state of consciousness is any state of awareness that differs from ordinary waking consciousness (alert, normal, waking state). Altered states can be intentionally induced through meditation, prayer, hypnosis, yoga and the ingestion of drugs, including alcohol and listening to music.

Altered states can come about accidentally, ex: a fever, sleep deprivation, fasting, oxygen deprivation, psychosis, epilepsy or a traumatic accident.

The human brain emits brain waves that move at various speeds. When we are fully awake and engaged in various activities, the brain operates on Beta wave state or Beta rhythm. The Beta state also occurs when anxious or in a drug induced condition. Many people do not do well in test situations because they are in a high state of Beta activity. This can cause anxiety, which can shut down the flow of information. Allowing students a short period of time to quiet the brain can result in getting beyond the stress of test taking and being able to concentrate on what they have learned about the subject being questioned.

The Alpha wave state occurs when we are idle, pondering or daydreaming. We are able to relax our mind and body in the Alpha wave state; therefore it is conducive to meditating. Watching TV can put us in an Alpha state; it is like taking drugs as it lowers brain function. It is why some people get addicted to watching TV.

Our aim is to slow down the brain's activity in order to achieve an altered state of mind that will allow us to focus our attention. The result is a condition in which we can relax our mind as well as our body as a means to begin a connection to our inner self.

Mind/Body Connection

Science based articles resulting from years of studies and research into the body-mind connection include analysis of the mechanism behind body-mind connection. The subject matter of these studies covers a wide range from employing meditation to fight cancer to the conclusion that Shakespeare was a master at portraying profound emotional upset through the physical symptoms of his characters.[1]

In a July, 2008 article in Science Daily, entitled *Mechanics Behind the Mind-body Connection*, scientists at UCLA cited that they had gained fresh insight by identifying how chronic emotional stress wears down the immune system. The study revealed that stress makes people susceptible to illness, especially those under long-term stress.[2]

With an estimate that 90% of disease is caused or complicated by stress, it is clear that physical health is directly affected by our emotional well-being. Meditation can free the mind from distress and irritation.

Actually, meditation is a process of un-learning rather than learning. At birth, our minds begin to be conditioned. The mind needs to be disciplined to support our efforts to subdue our thoughts. Again, this takes practice. Be cautious that your expectations are not too high, especially at first and that the length of the meditations are not too long. If you feel that you cannot maintain your focus and you are getting fidgety, it is time to stop and try again later.

Metaphysicians have taught and spoken out for centuries about the connection and ability of the mind to influence the body. Meditation has been practiced since ancient times as a component of numerous traditions and beliefs. Buddhist Monks included awareness in their day to day activities as a form of mind training. Yoga, Tai Chi and Qi Gong are all forms of moving meditation.

The truth is that we actually *can* learn to meditate while engaging in our daily activities. We can train our mind to be able to meditate anywhere and anytime. We can slip into a meditative state while doing the dishes or walking the dog. I tell my students that they can learn to meditate on a New York City subway at rush hour. The key is tuning out all the extraneous voices, noises and commotion going on around us. Imagine being able to find a peaceful place no matter what is happening. Not easy, but well worth the effort to accomplish.

Many of the finding of medical research on mind-body connection have made their way into main-stream medical practices. The traditional medical community is becoming increasingly open to exploring partnerships with holistic forms of ministering to the ill and injured, such as acupuncture, sacral cranial therapy, body message and energy therapy, in particular, Reiki. (more on Reiki in this chapter)

Many respected journals and magazines have published articles about meditation. According to a recent article in *The Chronicle of Higher Education,* , *People who meditate and focus on breathing are better able to concentrate on their immediate tasks, in other words will do better in school.*[3]

Some colleges have recently added meditation to their programs. The University of Massachusetts Amherst holds weekly meditation groups which are available to all students, as well as offering meditation during finals week.

The integration of meditation techniques in school curriculum or simply allowing students a few minutes of quiet time to reduce their mind's activity can result in not only greater achievement in reaching academic success but can lead to an enriched and enjoyable education experience.

The same practice for teachers would create a more relaxed atmosphere to prepare for the day, for both teacher and student and at the same time, build a stronger connection to each other.

Benefits of Meditation

Meditation focuses your attention, activates your power and increases your connection to your senses. This allows greater proficiency in performing your job and hobbies, and a deeper enjoyment of relationships retaining a sense of clarity for problem solving.

- Meditation is not connected to religion, but creates a deeper sense of the self.

- Meditation keeps the mind in the present moment.

- Meditation has a yin and yang component, the masculine and feminine; the yin being receptive awareness, openness, expansion and receiving and the yang represents focus, power and concentration.

- Meditation is a means to survive and live well in the fast-paced, sometimes chaotic environment of the 21st century.

- Meditation suppresses depression, manages pain, reinforces the immune system and lowers blood pressure. It has become significant in creating and maintaining good physical and emotional well-being.

The Dalai Lama on the benefits of meditation:

Achieving genuine happiness may require bringing about a transformation in your outlook, your way of thinking and this is not a simple matter. In taking care of your physical body, you need a variety of vitamins and nutrients, not just one or two. In the same way, in order to achieve happiness, you need a variety of approaches and methods to deal with and welcome the varied and complex negative mental status. It is not possible to accomplish that simply by adopting a particular thought or practicing a technique once or twice. Change takes time. As long as there is a lack of inner discipline that brings calmness to the mind, external facilities or conditions will never give you the feelings of joy and happiness that you are seeking.

The Journey Into Silence: how meditation unfolds

There are many types and styles of meditation. I am presenting a simple formula, one that anyone can follow and with practice, can be successful in a relatively short time.

First, conduct an inventory and assessment of your perceptions, attitudes and beliefs about life, your life, in particular. The release of any expectation for a perfect life is essential. There is no such thing. We learn valuable life lessons through the challenges that are set before us and the key to learning the lessons is how we respond to them.

There needs to be a shift of perspective to release any negative attitudes. Lowering expectations as to outcomes is essential. Without creating a positive state of mind, the benefits of mediation will be, at best, minimal.

To achieve a meditative state it is important to learn to accept that you are a whole and good person. How we view ourselves is important, as it is in meditation that we connect on a deep level to our true self.

There are 4 stages of meditation in this example:

Relaxation: to quiet the mind and body to create a feeling of balance and peacefulness in order to bring about rhythmic breathing and slow down brain activity.

Intention: what do you want to accomplish in this meditation; reduce stress, ponder a problem or concern or simply bask in the peaceful silence?

Connection: creating a state of awareness that will allow you to focus on your intention.

Return: a means to end the meditation and return to a feeling of balance.

Let me walk you through each stage before I give you a meditation to try.

Relaxation: begin by finding a comfortable place to sit. Some people can meditate while lying down, but I find that it is best to begin your practice by sitting in a chair. You don't need unusual positions, such as a lotus position; just remember to keep your spine straight as you can without being uncomfortable, as a straight spine helps your energy to flow and aids breathing by opening up more space in your lungs. Relax your arms and legs and place your hands on your knees with palms facing up. This will activate the natural Ki energy of the body. Ki energy is a force that governs human body functions. It is also called life force. It is the central underlying principle in traditional Chinese medicine and martial arts and Reiki.

Begin to relax every part of your body beginning with your feet. In your mind, visualize this energy entering your body through the soles of the feet and slowly moving up your body, stopping briefly at the ankles, knees, hips, lower organs, abdomen, chest area, throat, mouth, ears, eyes, forehead and finally the top of the head. You may need to adjust your body position slightly from time to time until you feel your body begin to relax. If you are familiar with the body's chakra system, bring the energy into each chakra. (see chapter twelve)

Begin to focus your attention on your breathing. Take a few deep, slow breaths, relaxing a little more with each out-breath. Let it flow, do not force, just allow your breath to flow gently in and out. Continue to be aware of your breathing until it evolves into a natural rhythm without effort.

Many people find it helpful to recite a mantra or a single word spoken at a steady rhythm such as the word "om." The mantra can be said out loud or in the mind. Counting your breaths also works with many beginners.

To further assist relaxing, discard and release any expectations you may have about your meditation competence, mostly by not expecting immediate results. Let the experience unfold in a soothing, easy manner.

Intention: intention needs to be decided before entering into a meditation. Think about how you want to use your time.

Connection: calling upon your intention or reason for this meditation, begin to become aware of the state of consciousness that you have created. Utilize all of your senses to allow your body to open to feeling that you are in a safe, peaceful place. Spend a few minutes in silence in these feelings.

Let thoughts float gently in your mind. The more you try to force them to stop, the longer they linger. If your mind begins to wander, simply invite your attention back to your breathing. Just becoming aware that your mind is wandering *is a success*.

When you feel that you can focus your attention to your purpose begin to reflect on your intention.

Return: when you begin to feel that you want to end your meditation, gradually begin to shift your awareness to your physical surroundings and gentle open your eyes. Take a few minutes to reflect on your meditation experience and records any thoughts, images, sounds, or colors you may want to remember.

The following is a basic, undemanding meditation to try. It is written in guided meditation format. It would be helpful to have someone read it to you, which would make it easier to go through the steps sequentially without the distraction of reading it to yourself.

- Set aside everything that might be a distraction...sit comfortably with your feet on the floor...hands on your knees...palms upward... your spine is straight, but not uncomfortable.
- You begin to relax and start to filter out thoughts that try to enter your mind...let it happen naturally. As your body begins to relax... the mind starts to become still .Use your inner vision...see all thoughts that still remain float out into the universe and disappear.
- Relax.
- Breathe in and out in a rhythmic pattern. With each breath that you exhale...feel that you are breathing out all stress...relax your mind and body. Feel a deep, quiet level of consciousness...your shoulders relax...and soon you feel your whole body begin to lose its tension.
- Relax.
- A feeling of serenity spreads through your body...sit in this serenity for a moment...listen to the silence you have brought into being... you come into the softness of complete relaxation.
- Focus on the stillness...feel an energy begin to come into your body through the soles of your feet. Know that you can trust this energy to move through you, because you have inspired it and created it-it is your energy. It comes from the highest part of who you are...it is safe to express your thoughts and rely on your inner vision.
- In your mind's eye, see the energy enter your body and begin to rise to the ankles and up the lower legs, relaxing the muscles.
- Bring the energy into the knees to allow it to sooth and heal.
- Permit the energy to enter into the lower organs to cleanse any impurities.
- Let the hip joints receive the energy to adjust any imbalance.
- With a deep breath allow the energy to fill the abdomen, to calm and heal any negative emotions or unrest.
- Permit the energy to fill the heart area to bring harmony and peace.

- The energy rises to the throat to bring wisdom to your words.
- It fills the mouth, ears and eyes, and rises into the crown of the head. This energy is a source of strength and will allow you to connect with your inner self.
- Draw this energy into your whole being and accept the thoughts and feelings of who you are, at your source.
- As you sit in this profound energy, begin your contemplation on your purpose for entering this peaceful silence…you feel the connection become solid and strong…notice the thoughts and images that come to you.
- It is time to return to this consciousness. Begin to become aware of your surroundings…when you are fully aware of your physical environment…gently open your eyes.

You may return to the center of your inner self any time you need to. Your feelings will become stronger each time and you will feel more stable and sure of yourself. Creating a serene environment is important to meditation, for some, candles add to a calm atmosphere. It is best not to eat before meditating as your body will be too busy digesting to relax. Soft music can help; sound affects brain waves and can calm the activity level of the mind. Listening to chants works for some, while others prefer total silence. Try different methods to assist your relaxation. Don't be discouraged if your mind resists attaining silence. Our minds are unruly and may swing back and forth between profound spiritual thoughts and what you need at the grocery store.

Try this very short, simple and effective centering meditation:

- Sit comfortably.
- Pay attention to your breathing, breathe deeply, but effortlessly.
- As you inhale, say the word "calm" in your head.
- As you exhale, say the word "now" in your head.
- Notice your breathing change and your body relax.

- Experiment with different times of the day until you find a time that seems favorable to relaxing and quieting your thoughts. Try to settle emotions before meditation. Anger and other negative emotions can lead to images in the mind that are difficult to restrain.
- Most of all, enjoy meditation, it is the quickest and easiest way to bring peace into your world.

CHAPTER TEN

What you love is a sign from your higher self of what you are to do.
Anaya Roman

THE HIGHER SELF:
get acquainted with the real you

The Higher Self? What does that mean? How many of me are there?

There is a finer part of each of us, a level of consciousness that encourages us to bring a greater purpose to our lives. It is called our higher self.

We all have different components to our personality. There is the person you are when in the company of strangers, the *you* with best friends, with your co-workers; the private *you* and the social *you*.

The higher self is the real you, it is the total soul consciousness. In other words, all that you have learned about your spiritual nature you have brought with you to this lifetime. It is the you that is living here on Earth. It is your deepest, spiritual self. It is where we reach into to write poetry or music or take in a sunset.

Our higher self gives us our insight, those flashes of feelings that tell us we are right. It is that still, small voice that urges us to do the right thing. We have all experienced hunches, feelings that something isn't right or logical or that what you are feeling is true. This is our higher self talking.

It speaks to us through our intuition. By the way, our intuition is *never wrong*. The word "intuition" is Greek in origin and means "protection." Our intuition is constantly trying to protect us from making negative or even unsafe choices. It is *us* that dismisses or ignores what our intuition is trying to say to us. Our higher self is connected to us and nothing can break that connection, even when we make choices that go against our basic beliefs, we still maintain full access to it. The key is to become comfortable and feel safe to seek the guidance of the higher self.

The higher self is our ultimate coach and supporter; always trying to help us to see all that we are and all that we can be. Because we have many components to our personality, we sometimes don't see our good works, especially when we are feeling wounded. In order to live life to the fullest expression, we must learn to know and accept ourselves for what we truly are, which is a divine being.

In order to heal beliefs that we are limited and damaged, we must choose to alter that belief, which is not easy work, but the rewards are significant. Higher Self is connected to us and nothing can break that connection.

We are continuously being swamped and sometimes overwhelmed by the needs of those around us: our parents, friends, family, co-workers and society in general and they all want to be heard.

How do we sort these voices out and decide which voice is coming from our higher self? Always remember that it is our Higher Self that is listening to these requests and in some cases, demands. Meditation is an excellent practice to enable you to connect to the higher self and it will be the only voice you will hear over the clamor of others. It is in meditation that we discover the soul and begin to live in a higher consciousness to realize and fully enjoy our birthright as a human being. This takes practice, but is part of the commitment to heal. (see chapter nine)

When we are in full connection with our personal core it becomes our closest companion, one that we can trust and depend on to never fail us.

Our Higher Self:

- keeps us attached to a path of spiritual growth
- helps us to achieve our highest potential to claim our power and abundance and to feel worthy to receive it.
- allows us to see that our "crooked" path of life is always for the best by helping us to see our issues and challenges from a different perspective
- helps us to love ourselves more and forgive others more, freeing us from the bonds of anger and resentment.
- teaches us to eliminate fear that inhibits our spiritual growth
- connects us to spiritual realms

- helps us to get where we need to be mentally, emotionally and spiritually.

The higher self will always encourage us, when we are faced with choosing the easy way or the hard way, to *always* choose the hard way. We grow best through the challenges of life. We are all seeking to find understanding of our true purpose for this earthly life.

We must come to realize that we really do have a part of ourselves that is always cheering us on and urging us to recognize that no matter what has befallen us along the way, that part of us is still intact and cannot be wounded by any life circumstance.

Higher Self Exercise: contract with your higher self.

We all enter into many contracts during the course of a lifetime ranging from a fairly minor verbal pact such as agreeing to take a turn at mowing the lawn to very complex, legal contracts with high stakes for either success or failure.

To enter into a contract with the higher self has the potential to raise your spiritual awareness.

Adapt any of this exercise to draw up a contract with your Higher Self. You may use these words verbatim or use your own words.

My contract with my Higher Self:

Because I am committed to increasing my self-assurance, in order to be the person I feel that I am, I pledge to do the following:

When thoughts or memories of negative or emotionally painful experiences begin to come into my mind, I will do my best to remember that it is not important what challenges I face, what matters is how I respond to them.

When I begin to doubt my ability to direct my life, I will call upon my inner wisdom to validate that I am capable of making choices that are for my highest good.

When this work of healing feels overwhelming and I am feeling that I am not worthy of a life beyond emotional pain, I pledge to call upon and listen to that part of me that will never abandon me, that only wants the best for me—my higher self.

You may sign and date it, if you wish.

Put your contract someplace that is easily accessible and check it from time to time to reread the pledge and assess how you are doing. You can feel free to alter any or all of them.

Note: Because we are human, our practices are not going to work all of the time. That's when we give ourselves a break, set it aside with a resolve to try again. One of the greatest of universal laws is that we are only charged with doing the best that we can.

Higher Self Worksheet

In your own words, from your heart, answers these questions with the first thoughts that come to mind. Do not analyze, second-guess or change too many times.

Tip: Try not to use extreme examples. Start with something simple. Ex: I will exercise once a week.

- What is a goal I would like to achieve?
- What blocks or fears do I have that would prevent me from attaining this goal?
- What skills or attributes do I have to help me attain this goal?

Is there a compromise to my goal in case it is not possible to achieve it at this time, so that I do not feel like a failure? Ex. If the opportunity to formally exercising once a week is not available, maybe a 15 minute walk could substitute. Remember goals happen in stages and sometimes they turn into something else you may want to do. It is fine to change goals along the way. The important part is to feel successful at making choices for yourself.

Identify an instance when you were faced with a challenge, no matter how trivial, when you used the higher part of yourself to face or solve the situation. Keep trying, there *is one*. This may be a question that you can leave and come back to later. (an opportunity to set a goal here to come back to this question)

CHAPTER ELEVEN

Be yourself; everyone else is taken.
Oscar Wilde

THE COURAGE TO BE YOU:
connecting with your power of courage

Your first act of courage was to be born on this planet

Each one of us has chosen to express ourselves as an individual. Our journey on Earth is learning how to use the qualities that we brought to this lifetime which are inherent in our human nature. Every act of courage that we carry out over the course of our lives becomes part of our spiritual history.

Most acts of courage were probably turning points in your life. The times when you took a step toward becoming what you instinctively knew you could be. They may have come about from a feeling of being encouraged from within yourself that you couldn't quite explain, but the feeling was strong enough that you moved forward in your pursuit of a change.

You may have done these things in spite of strong objections of your family and friends. You may have removed yourself from an environment that was pleasant and comfortable, but you felt that it had lulled you into a state where you sensed that you were not making any spiritual progress. Maybe you felt that your consciousness did not match what you were feeling within yourself and you began seeking new ways to expand your awareness to another dimension of who you are.

Some people move to another city or state, maybe without a job, money or family. A physical move often follows an expansion of consciousness. Ending or changing perspective on a relationship is common. Most people do not consider that ending a relationship can sometimes be the result of one partner expanding on a spiritual level and the other is not ready or is resistant to the shift. Sometimes adding a room to your house or creating a garden is a symbolic move. Even painting your front door a new color is a symbol of acknowledging who you are. Just the act of deciding to wear different colored clothing is saying, *I am different, I have changed.*

An interesting study conducted by Dr. Gregory Bern of Emory University in Atlanta, was entitled, *Why Do People Follow the Crowd?*[1]

Participants were asked questions about comparing geometric shapes. Most people answered correctly. However, when they were brought into a group that consistently and deliberately gave incorrect answers, the participants changed their previous correct answers to match the new group.

It makes sense from an anthropological point of view. We are tribal creatures and our survival, even today, depends on one another. One of our greatest fears as human beings is being alone, so we tend to go along with what others are doing, so that we feel that we belong. But, sometimes the courage to take your own road can make a difference between being who you came here to be and being just being another face in the crowd.

Traditional definitions of courage via the dictionary refer to bravery, boldness, fearlessness and fortitude. It goes on to say that courage is about the ability to confront fear, pain, danger and uncertainty. The third definition states: the mental or moral strength to venture, persevere and withstand danger, fear or difficulty by being willing to stand behind your beliefs. These define the various facets of courage.

While each of the meanings has an element of truth, the third definition comes closest to what is spiritual courage. It is about being willing to listen to your inner prompting to live deeper into your spiritual nature. Courage is innate and resides within us; it is an old French word meaning heart and spirit. We perform and witness acts of courage every day, but do not necessarily define them as such.

Spiritual courage involves taking risks. It is not about jumping over the Grand Canyon or going over Niagara Falls in a barrel. True they are called courageous acts, but they do not come from the inner self. Spiritual courage is completely different; it is following our heart at the risk of losing the respect of others.

*Live your beliefs and you can turn your world around....*Thoreau

Being who you are is hard work. It shouldn't be, but we humans tend to make things more difficult than they need to be. An important aspect is to allow others to help us, when needed. Trusting others creates a bond and mutual energy. We do not need to trust blindly; we need to assess who is trustworthy and who is not. Strengthening our intuition about others helps to gain confidence in our abilities to gather around us those who have our best interests at heart.

A key to realizing your potential is to examine your beliefs about miracles. They need not be so mysterious. The word literally means "to wonder at." Learn to get comfortable with the fact that they happen every day. Miracles are any occurrence that furthers us on our spiritual path.

There are small miracles and very powerful miracles, from finding that fifty cents you need on the bottom of your purse to recovering from cancer. However, in order for a miracle to occur, we have to "get out of the way" by not insisting that things have to be met in a certain way or that only one person can give us what we need. We can actually block a miracle from occurring by being too attached to *how* things should happen. Letting go of expectations and just allowing the universe to generate what we really need, can create a limitless potential for miracles.

An interesting activity involving miracles is to keep a "miracle journal." For a period of time that you determine, record each day something that you consider to be a miracle, based on the definition above; something unexpected that came into your life; or you can ask for something that you want and pay attention if it came to you and by what means. Remember, what we ask for does not always come in the form that we have requested, but it will come in the form of what we need. Doing this simple exercise can help greatly to identify the many ways opportunities and gifts come into our lives, many of them going unnoticed or dismissed. It takes courage to look for miracles and perhaps look at them from a different point of view. Knowing that miracles happen for us all the time is life changing and prompts us to adopt a greater degree of gratitude.

We are who we are by design, not by accident. Who we are is our soul's choice; how and where we live, our strengths, talents and abilities, our family of origin, the circumstances of our birth, our career path, our friends, lovers and children. All of these details are right for us at this time of existence and are all part of coming to know our infinite spiritual character, no matter what conditions or circumstances come into our lives.

We make choices, to go with or against our basic nature. The greatest choice we can make as humans is to follow our instincts to become the best we can be in this lifetime. We live in harmony with our inner self by accepting the responsibility that we have chosen to experience this life and all the rewards and difficulties that are part of it.

Spiritual courage is giving yourself permission to act, no matter what others may say or think. That is not an easy task. It involves trusting your intuition even when others do not agree with your decisions.

It also means conquering the fear that arises and tries to get us to go against our inner convictions, even when we know it is not the path we want to follow. Many people choose partners, careers, locations to live and other important life decisions that should come from the soul, just to please someone else. *So often times it happens that we live our lives in chains and we never even know we have the key.* (Eagles) [2]

When we realize that each of us can be unique and still be part of the rest of the world, is when we begin to live our lives through spiritual courage.

The new kids do not lack spiritual courage; in fact their capacity to show spiritual courage is at the very foundation of their frustration. Many of them do not live in an environment that supports or encourages their need to follow their own path. Fighting the social and education systems in which they find themselves, only serves to heighten their sense of isolation and judgment of their often perceived odd behavior.

If we are to create a new society, a new way of living in harmony with ourselves and others, these new kids need the latitude, and our help, to build their own road to the future. This can only occur, in large part, by significant and fundamental revisions in our current education structure that gives them the freedom to move us all forward into a new way of conducting this experience we call life on this planet.

CHAPTER TWELVE

The body never lies.
Martha Graham

A BIT ABOUT CHAKRAS:
why the New Kids need to know about them

Our Bodies Have Been Designed to be Self-Renewing and Self-Healing.

The western view of the chakra system was developed and explained by C.W. Leadbeater, a pioneer in metaphysics and theosophy, in his 1927 book *The Chakras*[1]

Chakras are electric energy centers which are created by the endocrine glands and the nerve centers in the body. There are hundreds of chakras in the body but traditional western teaching begins with the study of the seven main chakras that run along the center of the body from the bottom of the spine to the top of the head. Each one is associated with a specific area of the body.

The word "chakra" is a Sanskrit word for wheel or circle. They are described as turning wheels of light. Some disciplines depict them as looking like a lotus flower. They create a pathway of spinning energy along the center of the body, each related to the other. Each chakra is represented by a color.

Chakras can go in and out of alignment (balance) depending on everyday highs and lows of one's life. When our energy system is not working in some way, messages are sent to our conscious level that something is wrong. Stressors of life, minor illnesses, emotions and even thoughts can change the equilibrium of the chakra system. They are influenced by *everything* that you do.

When you are feeling anxious, unwell or not following your path in life, your chakras may shift way out of alignment and if left untreated/unbalanced, can take a long time to regain balance.

We need to always remember that the human body is an electromagnetic system. A healthy balanced chakra has energy flowing through it. Where there is disease (dis-ease), the body is not in a state of "ease" or wellness and the energy of the chakra becomes slow or even blocked. When a chakra energy flow is blocked physical and emotional illnesses can occur. When chakras are balanced they promote the elimination of negative thoughts and perceptions and allow one to live as a healthier, more empowered person.

There are many ways to align and balance chakras including, but not limited to: using the properties of crystals that relate to each chakra, energy work, such as Reiki, reflexology, color therapy, meditation and eating certain foods.

Our other energy field is our aura or force field which surrounds the human body as well as all living things on Earth. Some people have developed their ability to see auras and aura energy has been photographed by a process called Kirlian photography, developed by an electrical engineer, Semyon Kirlian in 1939. It is a form of contact print photography associated with electrical energy. The energy field of the body is reflected in the photograph by the colors of the chakras present around the person at the moment of the photograph, producing a colorful halo or aura.

Our aura is not separate from our chakras as they work in tandem with each other. Our energy flows from the body, through the chakras, into our aura and out into the outside world. In reverse, energy from the outside world comes into our aura and into our chakras, which is why events taking place around us can affect how we are reacting and feeling, which in turn, affects our body's energy.

Because the functions of the chakras are linked to the physical, emotional and mental expressions of the body, it is essential that students have healthy, balanced energy centers. For example the crown chakra (7th) is connected to mental acuity and the brow chakra (6th) is connected to the pineal gland, that produces melatonin, which regulates sleep and waking up; both vital to a successful and enjoyable school career.

The following is a synopsis of each chakra, its function, color, connection to areas of the body, positive expressions and effects of misalignment and unbalance. As each account is read, it becomes quite clear that the energy centers of the new kids need to be healthy and strong; a significant factor in nourishing their physical, mental and emotional bodies and advancing their mission.

Instinctively they accept their energy centers, knowing that there is more to the human body beyond the physical senses. Searching outside of their basic knowledge about the human experience is central to their inquisitive minds and any information that can be brought to their attention to strengthen their intentions and determination will be more than welcome. This is the kind of insight that they are seeking from us and are not getting.

Alternative means of education, such as home schooling, could introduce the chakras as part of mind-body activities. Certainly, parents can acquaint themselves with the body's energy system, whether their children attend traditional schools or not, which could also greatly benefit them as well as their children.

Knowing about the chakra system and how to keep it healthy is one more way to enrich the lives of the new kids. They are engaged in a monumental task, which is helping the human race to evolve to the next dimension of life on Earth. They are trying to take us to where we need to be. We owe it to them to provide them with any and all support and a means to fulfill their goal.

This effort also comes under the heading of education and this is a manner of education that parents, relatives, friends and others have some control over, without the restrictions of mandates and standards. Teachers and others working within an education setting can also gain remarkably by learning how to keep the chakra system balanced to reduce stress to maintain a healthy body and positive outlook.

CHAKRAS: ASSOCIATIONS AND CONCEPTS [2]

1ST CHAKRA: BASE CHAKRA: RED

Endocrine gland: adrenals. Area(s) of body governed: spinal column, kidneys

- Sits at the base of the spine.
- It is our survival center, source of strength, determination, and

supports the nurturing of our friends and family, health, abundance, security, practical matters, traditions, endings and beginnings as well as our human potential.

- It is here that we experience our connection to the Earth.
- In certain traditions, is regarded as the resting place of kundalini (also called "chi," "ki" and "Reiki")
- A healthy base chakra will keep you grounded and help you to move forward in life.

HOW TO TELL WHEN YOUR BASE CHAKRA IS OUT OF BALANCE

A slow or blocked base chakra can lead to stagnation of life's movements… feeling stuck. A loss through death or a broken relationship when the emotions are not released can lead to dysfunction in this chakra.

Symptoms include:
chronic lower back pain, fertility issues sciatica, immune disorders varicose veins, feelings of insecurity, water retention, phobias constipation/diarrhea, depression, anxiety, panic attacks, rectal or anal problems

**Healing the base chakra is very important as it stimulates the body's whole energy system and has an effect on all other chakras by moving anxiety and releasing unwanted and unneeded emotions and thoughts that can block your life path and plan.

2nd CHAKRA: SACRAL CHAKRA: ORANGE

Endocrine gland: Gonads. Area(s) of body governed: reproductive system

- Located just below the navel in the lower pelvic region, called the sacral area.
- Center of creativity, stamina ,relationships ,joy, happiness, sexuality,

energy, confidence, contains the creative life force for existing in the physical world.

- It is our connection to other people…Some traditions say that this force is the basis for life itself.
- We store healthy energy here for future use when needed. It gets some energy from the base energy which is why it is important that the base chakras needs to be healthy.
- This energy that is stored is released naturally when the body needs it to increase stamina.
- The health of the sacral chakra is essential to both physical and spiritual balance

SIGNS OF OUT OF BALANCE SACRAL CHAKRA
chronic low back pain, kidney and urinary tract infections, sciatica, gall bladder disorders, GYN problems, impotence, menstrual cycle problems, lack of confidence, intestinal disorders, unbalanced emotions, spleen conditions, eating disorders

CHAKRA: SOLAR PLEXUS: YELLOW

Endocrine gland: pancreas. Area(s) of body governed: stomach, liver, gall bladder, nervous system

- Located in the middle of the body, just below the breastbone, where the ribs are joined together in the front of the body.
- It is the seat of our emotions.
- The center of our personal power, ambition, desires, feelings and our sense of touch and our spiritual growth is processed through the solar plexus (gut feelings)
- As it is in the center of the body, it is the point of centering where we come to stillness. Essential in mediation to still the solar plexus as well as the mind.
- When healthy, this chakra produces a protective and cleansing

energy that flows out through our energy system (including the aura) dispersing any negativity being held in any of the other chakras. (when one is affected, they are all affected)

- Is related to the metabolic and digestive systems and to the pancreas for the conversion of food. It is important to diabetics to keep the solar plexus chakra healthy.
- It is the site of our "internal pendulum" our instinctive yes/no response.
- When healthy you become aware of how you feel about the world and events around you.
- When out of balance, will feel drained, this chakra is greatly affected by stress.

SIGNS OF OUT OF BALANCE SOLAR PLEXUS CHAKRA

lack of concentration, digestion disorders, failing memory, eating disorders, falling asleep during the day, stress related skin conditions, insomnia

4TH CHAKRA: HEART CHAKRA: GREEN

Endocrine gland: thymus. Area(s) of body governed: heart, blood, vagus nerve, circulatory system

- Located in the *middle* of the chest (spiritual heart, not physical)
- Relates to your connection to everyone and everything around you... the key concept of love and relationships.
- Without this connection we are unable to share the love we have within us.
- It is the deepest point inside us, where the outside world meets our inner being. Is the site of the balance between our spiritual and human side.
- With each breath we take we inhale part of the outside world and we exhale our internal energy to the space and people around us.
- Key words of the heart are safety, trust, commitment, forgiveness,

compassion, hope, seeing beauty, harmony, adventure, relationships, and sleep. (when the heart is at peace, peaceful sleep will occur)

- Also the chakra where the prompting and passion to teach others originates.

SIGNS THAT HEART CHAKRA IS OUT OF BALANCE
emotional confusion, chest, lung and respiratory disorders, unloving and uncaring attitude asthma, repeated colds and flu, narrow-mindedness, early physical signs of aging, relationship breakdown, many unrelated symptoms, one after the other, heart disease

5TH CHAKRA: THROAT CHAKRA: BLUE

Endocrine gland: thyroid. Area(s) of body governed: bronchial and vocal mechanisms, lungs, alimentary canal

- Located in the middle of the neck above the collar bone, covers the area of the throat and ears.
- The center of communication and expression.
- Not only verbal communication, but physical (body language) and mental contact (telepathy) as well as the written word.
- Tells the world how we feel and expresses our beliefs and share the teaching we all have to give. Key words: Communication, expression, willpower, addiction, choice, freedom, faith, ability to make decisions, through communication.
- When out of balance, can lose our focus easily and affects creativity.
- Emotional trauma can have great affect on the throat chakra. (abused children)
- The brain's reasoning processes can be obstructed and can also lead to speech impediments.

SIGNS THAT THROAT CHAKRA IS OUT OF BALANCE
skin rashes, fear of speaking your mind, heart attack, lack of concentration,

weak or bad back, attention deficit disorders, digestive problems, feelings of unease, anxiety, IBS (Irritable Bowel Syndrome), Crohn's disease

6TH CHARKA: BROW CHAKRA: INDIGO

Endocrine gland: pituitary. Area(s) of body governed: lower brain, left eye, ears, nose, nervous system

- Also known as the 3rd eye, is located in the middle of the forehead, between and slightly above the above the eyebrows.
- It is the center of intuition, intellect, personal magnetism, our inner vision and perception.
- Is the center where creativity and inspiration combine. Psychic abilities and gifts are also focused here.
- When healthy and balanced helps to remove negativity and selfish attitudes and facilitates intuition and wisdom.
- When dysfunctional the mind can become unbalanced and negative ideas may set in and thoughts can become rambling and disoriented.
- Can inhibit our creative paths and cause our awareness to diminish and we can also lose touch with our senses causing our physical abilities to suffer.
- May feel blocked to new ideas and feel stuck in an emotional and mental rut. In extreme cases, mental illness can set in.

SIGNS THAT 3RD EYE CHAKRA IS OUT OF BALANCE
mental illness, eye conditions, headaches and migraines, learning disability, personality disorders, feelings of negativity, sinusitis, lack of ambition

7TH CHAKRA: CROWN CHAKRA : VIOLET

Endocrine gland: pineal. Area(s) of the body governed: upper brain, right eye

- Located at the top of the head, it is the center of spirituality, enlightenment and dynamic thought.

- It facilitates the flow of wisdom to you from the universe and connects you to the consciousness to all that is.

- When healthy and balanced, helps you to distinguish between truth and illusion.

- Helps you to see how to balance the spiritual with the physical world.

- Helps to eliminate pride and vanity.

- Allows you to detach yourself from emotions and express genuine self-awareness.

- Helps you to see the bigger picture, it is your connection to the angels and your potential.

SIGNS THAT YOUR CROWN CHAKRA IS OUT OF BALANCE

ME (Myalgic Encephalitis), skin conditions, depression, dementia nervous system disorders, vanity[2]

Foods to Help Keep Chakras Balanced.

1st chakra: red foods; beets, red fruits and vegetables
2nd chakra: orange foods; oranges, carrots, seeds, nuts
3rd chakra: yellow foods; yellow peppers, corn, pineapple, brown rice
4th chakra: green foods; broccoli, leafy greens
5th chakra: blue foods; blueberries, blue raspberries
6th chakra: violet foods; purple potatoes, blackberries, blueberries
7th chakra: purple foods; plums, eggplant, purple grapes

CHAPTER THIRTEEN

When you heal yourself and assist others with their self-healing, you heal the Earth.
Laural Steinhice

REIKI: The Ancient Healing Art.

What Has Reiki to Do With the New Kids?—Everything.

We live in a time of accelerated change and personal and planetary evolution. Many of the shifts are resulting in chaos in all aspects of our lives. The Earth itself is also in a physical crisis with increased numbers of hurricanes, earthquakes, droughts, tornadoes and floods.

As the old is making way for the new, there is an increased recognition for the need for change and a new awareness is being born.

We live in a time when many are asserting their power that has been overtaken by the few. A new sense of freedom of human development is emerging. The metaphysical New Age movement has offered awareness and inner growth to an increasing number of people.

Traditional medicine has been under scrutiny by some who question excessively high fees, over medication and the control by insurance and drug companies. Many people have turned to holistic methods to address illness and injuries.

There is a major interest in the resurgence of non-invasive methods that were used in the past to assist the human body to heal, such as massage, acupuncture, essential oils, herbs and therapeutic touch; approaches that have proven to be effective, some thousands of years.

Reiki, a therapeutic touch, is a most important holistic technique that continues to grow as a significant and respected remedial practice. It requires no tools or equipment except the practitioners hands, can be administered on short notice, it is easily taught and everyone, including children, can use and benefit from it.

Dolores R. Card, Hermon R. Card

The Story of Reiki

The exact date of origin of Reiki cannot be determined. Before written records were kept, information about Reiki was passed down through the ages through anecdotes and verbal testimonies. However, accounts of Reiki extend over all written records of humanity. Modern era history of Reiki began in the mid 1800s. Mikao Usui, is credited with bringing forth the principles of Reiki. While living on a Zen Buddhist monastery in Japan, he found texts written in Sanskrit describing the healing formula of Reiki. Because he had studied Sanskrit, Usui was able to translate the 2500-year-old system of healing.

It is said that the children of early Earth received Reiki I training at the beginning of grade school age and Reiki II at what we consider junior high or middle school age. Reiki III, the Teacher/Master training was required for all educators.

Reiki was mostly kept secret and only allowed to be practiced in Japan to citizens of Japan. One needed to be invited to participate in Reiki training, as well as pay the high cost of the required fee.

A successor of Usui, Hawayo Takata brought the practice and teaching of Reiki to the Western world in the 1940s. Although Usui Traditional Reiki (also called Usui Reiki Ryoho) was taught, teaching techniques and methods have undergone changes and several branches of Reiki have evolved; the Usui method is the closest to what Hawayo Takata brought from Japan. All methods work and all have evolved from Hawayo Takata's teachings.

The origins of Reiki need to be honored and respected. At the same time we need to recognize the changing world and the distinctive needs of the current population of the Earth.

How Does Reiki Work?

The discovery of the existence of the human energy field has dramatically changed the views of mainstream biomedical science.

As far back as the 1920s and 1930s, Harold Saxon Burr, a distinguished researcher at Yale University suggested that diseases could be detected before physical symptoms appeared. Burr was convinced that diseases could be prevented by altering the energy field. More recent research has shown that cells and tissues in the human body generate a magnetic field that can be detected. These discoveries are being confirmed due to the development of sensitive instruments that can detect the minute energy fields in and around the human body. These research results have led to an understanding of the role of energy fields in health and disease. Actually, nothing is solid. Everything on Earth has an aura of energy surrounding it.

Reiki is life force energy. This energy is transmitted through the hands of the Reiki practitioner by utilizing the energy fields of the human body. Everyone has the capacity to perform Reiki. Energy can flow through the hands at other times when not focusing on Reiki.

Reiki In The Modern World

In varying degrees in the medical community, Reiki is considered to be an effective method to attend to the ill. It is considered to be complementary health care, valuable as an addition to, not a substitute for traditional health care.

In the past 10 years, the use of Reiki has increased among nurses, physicians and rehabilitation therapists in hospital settings, hospice care, emergency departments, psychiatric settings, nursing homes, operating rooms and family practices.

Nurses report, through clinical observations, that the practice of Reiki with patients has relaxation effects, stress reduction benefits, aids pain management and helps to alleviate the anxiety of patients' family members. Reiki is also used in some hospital and hospice programs in conjunction with palliative care for patients.

Many hospitals across the United States have integrated Reiki programs managed by hospital staff or Reiki practitioners from the community. Some chiropractic offices employ Reiki as a complement to their practice. As animals are very aware of Reiki energy and can also benefit from its affects on pain reduction, Reiki is available in some veterinarian practices.

More Facts About Reiki:

Reiki, is very gentle and never causes pain and cannot be misused or used for negative effects. It is a source of comfort by releasing emotional trauma as well as helping the body to relieve pain and hasten physical healing.

- Although spiritual in nature, it is not a religion.
- Reiki can be used to help people at the time of their death and can help with the grieving process for family and friends.
- Reiki can be used to help us engage more deeply in the world around us and is a valuable tool for the quest for spiritual growth.
- Reiki can help with menopausal symptoms and insomnia.
- Reiki can help to release stored up toxins from the body.
- Reiki can be used during childbirth to lower anxiety and reduce pain.
- Chemotherapy patients have reported that they noticed a marked decrease in side effects from treatments with the use of Reiki.
- Reiki can be sent long distance, to individuals, groups or out into the world to promote peace and harmony for the Earth.
- Reiki can be given to the self to promote healing in mind, body and spirit.

Becoming a Reiki Practitioner: Reiki training

Training for Reiki practitioners first must include the history of Reiki for an understanding of how the practice evolved.

Reiki Level I

Reiki is usually divided into three levels of instruction. Level one is an introductory training where the basics of Reiki are taught. Detailed instruction about how Reiki energy is generated and passed through the hands to another's body, as well as opportunities for practice are an essential part of the training. Specific ways to hold the hands while performing Reiki, called hand positions, are demonstrated by the teacher, and again, the student is encouraged to practice. Students are paired with each other as a means to practice.

At each level of training an attunement, which is an initiation done during a brief ceremony by the teacher, opens up the body's energy channels. This allows the Reiki energy to transmit from the practitioners hands to others. The attunement does not give the student Reiki—it opens and aligns what is already there. Remember, we all come equipped with Reiki energy; it is part of our genetic heritage.

Reiki Level II

Reiki II increases self-awareness and the realization that we are responsible for our lives and have free will choices about what manifests in our lives. There is also a consciousness for the need to channel our energies in positive ways.

Level II instructs the student to the use of Sacred Reiki Symbols, brought down through the ages, which are used for deeper physical and emotional healing, as well as the ability to send Reiki energy over distances. The Tibetan Monks and Lamas originally used the Reiki symbols for meditation purposes as a means to increase spiritual enlightenment. Practice using the Reiki symbols is an essential part of level II training.

The concepts that Reiki can be used to reduce stress, alleviate fears and promote the healing of addictive behaviors as well as other forms of emotional distress, are introduced at this level and further developed in level III.

Ability to send and receive intuitive message is greatly enhanced by the Level II attunement, as it helps to stimulate the intuitive center of the brain, which is located in the pituitary gland. Science recognizes that the pituitary gland to be the mechanism by which we receive mental vibrations.

Reiki Level III: Master/Teacher Level

Motivation for being certified as a Reiki Master/Teacher varies. Some simply want to complete the three levels for their own enlightenment. Many people want to be able to use Reiki to help friends and family. Some want to establish themselves as Reiki practitioners either in a private practice or connected to a metaphysical or medical facility and some want to take on the responsibility to create much needed new Reiki teachers.

A large part of this level concentrates on the responsibilities of a Reiki Master/Teacher, including a code of ethics that is inherent to the practice of any spiritual work that are impressed upon the students.

The essentials of teaching Reiki are defined and discussed. The symbols used in Level III are assigned and practiced.

Students learn the body's chakra system and the importance of integrating them into the practice of Reiki. They also learn how to pass attunements to others, especially important to those who will become Reiki teachers. Students also receive their third degree Reiki attunement.

Many Reiki teachers are now adding supplemental information to include:

- Balancing chakras with crystals
- Scanning for physical and emotional blocks
- Reiki for specific illnesses: ex. migraines, back pain, cancer
- Using a pendulum with Reiki
- Reiki with animals

There are many methods of therapeutic touch, all valuable and beneficial. The important point, no matter which method you are drawn to, is that these practices are all a form of service to humanity.

The New Kids and Reiki

Reiki can be an essential part of planetary healing. The call to action is already being answered by the new kids to show us the way to the fifth dimension of human consciousness. They are naturally attuned to Reiki energy. They are going to need all the support we can give them to accomplish this. Bringing Reiki into their lives at an early age is a way to help them to keep their chakras aligned and healthy in order to handle all the turmoil around them as they forge this path. Practicing Reiki can also channel their high energy and extreme emotions in positive directions and ease the stress of their work. Because Reiki energy is second nature to them, as they become adults, many will choose to become Master/Teachers, perpetuating a culture that lives by the five Reiki principles:

Just for today, I will give thanks for my many blessings.
Just for today I will not worry.
Just for today I will not be angry.
Just for today I will do my work honestly.
Just for today I will be kind to my neighbor and every living thing.

Reiki is an important return to the ancient past and comes from cultures where compassion and oneness prevailed, which are the basis of Reiki. In this present time of the transformation of humanity, Reiki can bring peaceful meaning back to the minds and hearts of all who inhabit this planet.

SECTION FOUR

ALTERNATIVE EDUCATION
ECHOES AND REFLECTIONS: voices of students and teachers
ENDING THOUGHTS

...only a job

Those of us who are lucky,
have passion in our life.

Passion for our family,
for our alma mater
our team
our pets
our lover,
our other.

We have passion for
politics, religion,
causes of import
issues of conscience,
the rose bush
we planted last week.

And we teachers have passion
for all those things,
and one thing more.

I could say that
we have passion for
our occupation,
our profession,
our chosen field,
for what we do,
and a dozen other euphemisms
that all imply
that teaching is work.

And of course it *is* work,
work that frustrates us,
confuses us,
saddens us,
angers us,
drains us,
wears us down to nearly nothing.

It is work
that makes us weep
for all we cannot do.

But, it is also work that
encourages us
enlightens us
delights us
amuses us
energizes us
turn us into giants…

Work that makes us celebrate
all that we do,

or else it's only a job.

…or else it's only a job.
Herm Card 2006

CHAPTER FOURTEEN

Every student can learn, just not on the same day, or the same way.
George Evans

ALTERNATIVE EDUCATION

Alternative education is a modification of traditional classroom settings and teaching methods. While these systems may include education designed for students with special needs, they have also been developed out of dissatisfaction with certain aspects of long-established educational philosophies.

But First, a Brief History of Systems of Schooling (and other interesting information)

The concept of learning spans millions of years; education a few thousand years, while the right to education and formalized instruction based on curriculum spans little more than a century.

Early civilizations instructed the young with the knowledge and skills they would need to survive, and passed the information on to the next generation. As cultures evolved, people began to depend on this practice of transmitting knowledge. At the time, it was passed on orally and by imitation. When the written word was developed the depth and scope of the knowledge greatly increased and now it could also be preserved. When the need for greater capabilities for communication and higher degrees of skills was recognized, what was considered schooling was developed. Schooling in this sense was already in place in Egypt in 3000 B.C.

Down through the ages, as each culture realized the importance of knowledge to maintain customs and traditions and improve their society, new subject matter and fields of study were added according to the needs of the population.

The greatest leap of educational development occurred during the Renaissance in Europe after the invention of the printing press. (Remember the new kid, Johannes Gutenberg?) Works of literature were now distributed across the continent and eventually across the globe. This advancement brought the emergence of a more constructive educational approach in the West.

The Philosophy of Education

We could write an entire book on the current philosophy of education, thought it is addressed throughout this work. Suffice it to say that the current philosophy of education is weighted to the concern about education policy and the skewed outward appearance of student success, instead of finding methods to bring out the best that each child can be.

What should be the current philosophy of education, was well stated by British philosopher, psychologist and educator John Locke (1632-1704) in *Some Thoughts Concerning Education*. His philosophical contributions opposed the scholastic method and harsh disciplines of the times. Although his recommendations of educational methods were for male students, they are relevant for females, as well. He favored an all-round, common sense education and he also paved the way for the field of child psychology. He emphasized the supportive relationship between teacher and student and the vibrant side of child life.

The following excerpts from his publication sound like they were written expressly for educating the new kids.

- Native propensities of children should be watched from the beginning, in order to discover the individual capacity for knowledge.

- Children are best able to develop their intellect and social skills through various kinds of play and the practice of certain skills, rather than the rote memorization of assorted rules.

- We must not hope to change their temperament. Children should study their nature and aptitudes and see by trial and error what turns they easily take and what becomes them.

- Make the best of what nature has given and give them all the advantages they are capable of.

- Everyone's natural intellect should be carried as far as it can, but to try to go beyond will be a labor in vain. Among those of equal education, there are great inequities of parts.

- There is frequently more to be learned from the unexpected questions of a child than the discourses of men.[1]

Insightful words from the 17th century! Not surprising, he was a stalwart supporter of home schooling and a forceful critic of institutional education.

Structured Education

Pre-K

It is well established that the most important years of learning begin at birth. During these early years, a human being is capable of absorbing more information than they will ever be able to again. The environment of the young child influences the development of cognitive skills and emotional fitness due to the rapid brain growth that occurs in the early years.[2]

In 1960 10% of the United States 3 and 4-year-olds were enrolled in some type of classroom. The first publicly funded preschool in the United States was created by President Lyndon Johnson in 1965.

In 2012, 75% of 3 and 4-year-olds are in a pre-school setting. These children are being served by programs that vary in enrollment, program design and operation. Lasting effects of pre-K education is mostly in learning social skills, interacting with others and learning to compromise, all important factors, not only in their academic careers, but in meeting life's challenges.[3]

Our youngest scholars of 2013 and beyond need to be listened to. Even at 3 and 4 years old, they like to have input into what is happening in their classroom environment to feel that they have choices, which helps them, in simple ways, to fit into the new ways of the world in which they were born.

Primary/Elementary

Usually a time-span of 6-8 years of schooling, starting at age 5 or 6, although ages vary between and within countries. Currently about 90% of elementary age children are enrolled in school.

Under the Education for All programs developed by UNESCO, most countries have committed to achieving universal enrollment in primary education by 2015. The average age to advancing to secondary schools is around the age of 14. Most school systems have separate middle or junior high schools.

Secondary/High Schools

High schools were not fully developed in the United States until 1910 when big business and technology advances in factories required skilled workers. High school curriculum at that time focused on practical job skills to meet the needs of this new kind of job demand. The primary goal was to prepare students for skilled blue collar work.

It also paved the way for higher wages for employees. Eventually, secondary education concentrated on preparing students for higher education or to train directly into a profession.

Education was filling the need of the times. Our current students are here to meet the demands of this high-tech age. However, their need to fulfill their goal is being compromised by their time and attention being diverted to preparing to take tests instead of preparing to embark on their life's work.

Guidance counselors were introduced in middle and high schools soon after the launching of Sputnik in October of 1957. The idea was to funnel more students into math and science in order to keep up with advances being made in other countries.

Diminishing Opportunities

Primary schools in Europe even before the 16th century offered apprenticeships to gain experience and skills in various trades working with masters of their craft. Students with an interest and a natural ability for working with their hands are finding it increasingly difficult to find classes and programs to enroll in. As a result, many students are dropping out of school due to limited academic choices that interest them and are opting to seek jobs that are not fulfilling or long-lasting. Where are our future plumbers, electricians, carpenters and other tradesmen to be trained?

Homeschooling

Before compulsory school attendance laws, most children were educated at home or within the community, primarily in local churches or community centers.

In recent years due to the growing dissatisfaction with education methods in the United States, so has the appeal of homeschooling increased. Since 1999 the number of children being homeschooled has increased by 75%. According to some statistics, there are more than two million children being educated in a home school setting.

Accurate statistic for the number of children being homeschooled are difficult to gather, due in part, that each state varies in their regulations such as registration, attendance mandates and reporting procedures.

The U.S. Department of Education publications maintain that most indicators show that the home school population has grown in undeniable terms during the past 3-5 years; suggesting that homeschooling is being chosen at an increasing rate, no matter what the conclusive stats are. There is no doubt that it is a growing trend and will continue to increase as people who were homeschooled in past years choose to educate their own children at home.

Parents cite numerous reasons to home school. The three main reasons given by the majority of parents who are homeschooling in the U.S. are:

- concern about the school environment
- desire to provide religious or moral values
- dissatisfaction with academic instruction in both public and private schools

Home schooling may also be a factor suitable to the choice of parenting style.

Home schools use a wide variety of methods and materials to educate. The major benefit for homeschooled children is the ability that parents, or others providing curriculum, have to discover what works best for the individual child, resulting in more than one approach can be experienced by the student.

The concept of natural learning is inherent in many home school methods that completely fit the philosophy of the kind of education our new kids need. Knowledge based on activities and experiences conducive to learning, but leaving them free to explore and learn as their interest leads.

Autonomous learning can also allow children to be partly responsible for their schooling. It helps them to develop confidence and promotes freedom of discussion. These new students have a strong need for independence and are naturally self-sufficient. They grow and thrive on self-directed accomplishments.

There is no reason that children who are homeschooled cannot learn as well as in public or private schools, providing that whoever teaches them are committed to the education process and are diligent about not only covering basic information about subjects, but to providing non-academic experiences needed for a well rounded education.

Home schooling is a lot of work. It is helpful if parents, or whoever is to home school, educate themselves about how to teach in an effective way. There are continuing education courses at some local colleges and universities to aid parents to "brush up" on the contents of many subjects or review the basic tenets of teaching.

Benefits of Homeschooling

There are numerous on-going debates about whether children are more successful in attending public or private schools vs. homeschooling. The reality is that there is no magic formula to assess this debate, especially given the characteristics of present-day students.

The main point toward supporting homeschooling is that the children we are calling new kids need the kind of latitude and a reliable environment to identify, explore and develop their potential for fulfilling their role in our changing society. Current public education has neither strategy nor the time to use these methods.

Children that are schooled at home have the opportunities to participate in real life challenges that arise. The family itself is a learning tool; its history, beliefs, value, patterns of interactions between other members, differences in perspectives about each role in the family and what that entails. Discussing the family rules and why they were set and explanations why certain rules cannot be changed can lead to learning to debate appropriately, to be a member of a group or team and to honor others' opinions in non-school settings. Working through difficulties that arise in every family is a life lesson that must be addressed whether a child is in a public, private or home school setting.

One of the main concerns about homeschooling is the socialization factor. The argument most often contended is that children need friends of their own age and that a parent should *never* take the place of a friend. Both of these concepts we strongly agree with.

These factors are often addressed by homeschooling advocates in these ways:

- There are special home school programs at museums, historical sites and nature centers. They are always looking for new ways to serve the public and are open to setting up specific home school programs that fit the need of the family, such as a night for teens to meet for board games, for example.

- There are also sports facilities in some communities that will allow homeschooled kids to participate in a sport or mentorship programs.

- Most communities have programs to enroll homeschooled students for group learning activities like field trips or art classes. Sharing lessons with other homeschooled kids provides very valuable social interaction.

- Some public schools allow homeschooled kids to participate in extra-curricular activities

- Teenaged homeschooled kids may find that they do not have enough interaction with kids their own age as it is a time when friendships are so important. There are so many more homeschooled kids now that some communities have information to connect them with each other.

- Typically, homeschooled kids play in varied age groups. Both boys and girls have the freedom to engage in play other than "socially acceptable" for their gender without fear of ridicule or being labeled.

- Homeschooled kids do not have to put up with bullying and other anti-social behavior.

- Socialization is not merely having a social life, but knowing how to act appropriately in various situations. Homeschooling parents have the opportunity to guide students towards a variety of activities that enhances their social development.

- A genuine and reliable advantage is the homeschooling network that is available and utilized by home school teachers that provides support, suggestions for and sharing of lessons, experienced guidance for beginners, a place to express frustrations and celebrate achievements and sometimes just to have like minded people to talk to.

Beyond the Curriculum

While most states and local school districts require that a curriculum be designed and submitted for approval, the advantage to home schooling is that you can go beyond what is required to construct a more individual approach to cover required subjects. Enlist the help of the children to formulate the curriculum. This is why the new kids make excellent home school students.

Everyone has a good supply of learning tools right in the home. Toys, for instance, acquired over the years, that speak to the interest of a child, can trigger a piece of writing or storytelling about why that particular toy or game was purchased. It could be an opportunity for a family discussion about family memories or why and how choices are made. New kids love to talk about choices.

Projects

There are many projects that can become either part of a curriculum or an adjunct activity. The following suggestions can not only be enjoyable, but have the potential to delve into a subject on a deeper and personal level. Hands on activities have a strong impact on strengthening critical thinking, creativity and problem solving skills. These activities can also address multiple subjects.

- Collect stories from relatives, especially grandparents and other older members of the family. All too often family names and information become lost, as the questions are not asked. Exploring family customs, where they came from and are they still being observed in the family can tie into customs of other countries' traditions. Discuss traditions the children might want to restore or bring into the family and a rationale why they might want to do this. Negotiate with other family members about suggestions. Would also make a great writing or journal exercise or creating a family history record to give as a gift for a special occasion.

- Students can "research" themselves through family discussions of their names. Knowing who named them and why can help develop a great sense of self and a feeling of connection to their family. By understanding the meanings, sources and unique nature of their names they can gain insight into family traditions, ancestry and history.

- Do a search at a library or on-line in other areas of the country the family has lived or local area if the family has always been in your present area. Note how each area was settled. Find pictures at local libraries or historical societies how the area looked like through the years. This kind of activity makes social studies and history very real and makes a personal connection to the student.

- Build a model, from Legos or toothpicks/popsicle sticks, of the family home. If you want a more ambitious project, a model of the neighborhood that could span over a school year. Choosing a time period to represent the neighborhood could add to the historical significance or include a store or business owned by a family member. To further promote pride in the project, consult with the local library to have it on display.

- Trace the history of schooling in the family by interviewing different generations about their experiences with their education. Make comparisons with different methods that were employed and make an assessment as to the most successful style of learning for each person interviewed and why.

- Globe/map hopping: study a globe or world map and choose countries or areas that seem to hold an interest for each child, even if they can't explain why they are drawn to that particular area. Investigate the country to try to determine what it is about the area that appeals to them.

- Make a plan for a family visit to a local historical society; a great opportunity for a history lesson and one that might be tied in to their own history.

- A planned trip to the grocery store to keep track of the prices of products and upon arriving home, add up products that were purchased. To further the activity, discuss the difference in prices of products as compared to other periods of time or items that come from different areas or other countries. An interesting aspect could also be how weather can affect food prices.

- If affordable, purchase a home school chemistry kit or make one from items that are used every day that you can buy from the supermarket, hardware store, or arts and crafts store. There are directions for kits for making almost everything on the Internet. The materials can be used for individual projects or group projects that promote compromise, collaborative planning and group decisions. If Internet is not available, most local libraries allow access to their computers.

- For older students, especially if they have narrowed down an interest in a specific career or vocation, arrange to interview a person or persons who are working in that occupation. Preparing for the interview will be part of the activity, including thinking over what questions they want to ask and planning what they want to share about themselves. Keeping notes, discussing their experience of the interview and their understanding of the information they received, can not only sharpen their skills of interacting with others, but can also be validating as to whether they still want to pursue that particular field.

- For older students , volunteering in their community can give them a sense of service to others as well as providing social interaction outside of the home.

- As students become old enough they may seek to find resources for learning on their own by conducting their own research, giving them a way to be involved in their education. Life skills and preparation for college can be accelerated by this independent aspect.

- Any activity that can be conducted out of doors. For example talking a walk to identify different trees and flowers, or sitting in a park to work on writing or reading assignment. These children want to be connected to nature in some way; it makes them feel part of the whole concept of the universe.

- There is a high correlation between music and math, as outlined in the *New Kids* chapter. If a child displays an interest or aptitude for playing an instrument, encourage them to try it on a trial basis, to see if they truly want to put the time and effort into learning to play it. A good activity involving music is to have each child identify what kind or kinds of music they enjoy listening to and have a discussion or have them write something about why that particular music calls their attention. Conduct a lesson where the kinds of music chosen are played and get comments and opinions from the group. Some older students might want to do research on a singing group, musician, or a specific song and its' meaning. Talk about how their choice in music might relate to their lives.

Robin, homeschooling parent of three children (has homeschooled in more than one state)

Homeschooling provides the wonderful opportunity to witness firsthand how learning takes place.

It is great experience to spontaneously discover something to study. Maybe it's a painting we saw on a trip to an art museum, a character in a book we are reading, or seeing a butterfly in the yard. There is never a lack of something to explore and it becomes an "instant" lesson.

We have the flexibility to expand on what needs to be covered in the required core subjects as we do not have strict time constraints to fit the lesson into a designated time frame. Learning becomes natural under these conditions.

Self-directed interests can lead to becoming aware of inherent talents of children. Homeschooling has pointed out what my children need to succeed in life.

There are countless ways to engage children in learning. Most of the ways can come from what is going on around them. One major component is curiosity. Trying to force kids into learning something can only result in tuning out that need to know, that is inherent in all of us.

All of the suggested projects are a means to generate and enhance a child's natural curiosity because they are student centered and have an individual component. New kids have a strong need to relate information and events to their own lives. They need to feel part of what is happening.

These same, or similar activities, need to be incorporated into public school curriculum for the same reasons. Even given that time is limited and certain subjects need to be addressed, some of these activities can be adapted, condensed or conducted over a period of time and some in conjunction with home work. This is not just a good idea, but necessary to connect current students with the original fundamental nature of education, which was to create whole, happy and productive human beings.

Some, of Many, Successful Alternative Schools:

The Jowonio School

Over 40 years ago, when the Jowonio School in Syracuse New York was founded, it was a unique venture in community education. Several parents, dissatisfied with the state of public education, pooled their educational resources to create what was essentially "group home schooling." The school focused on inclusion, and oddly enough, the inspiration was student driven, not agency mandated. The handful of autistic students had their own classroom, but the "typical" students soon migrated among them, creating an environment that made one wonder who was including whom?

The school continues to thrive as an inclusive pre-K school that has garnered community support and national recognition for its efforts to educate children by addressing their needs and abilities rather than their data.

www.jowonio.org/

The Montessori School Educating the Whole Child

Children have within them a natural urge to explore and discover the world around them and to find joy in learning when they are actively engaged in the learning process Dr. Maria Montessori

http:/www.montessorischool.net

Ami-usa@montessori.ami.org

Rudolf Steiner School

Our highest endeavors must be to develop free human beings, who are able of themselves to impart purpose and direction to their lives....Rudolf Steiner

http://www.steiner.edu

Rosetta Stone Homeschool (for language skills)

http://www.rosettastone.com

We are not advocating any specific system of education. The choice of schooling must be made through a means that fits and enhances the beliefs and philosophies of each family. We *are* advocating that whatever method is chosen, the needs of these new kids must be addressed. They must be provided the freedom to learn beyond the limitations of the current system.

CHAPTER FIFTEEN

Teaching is not a lost art, but the regard for it is a lost tradition
Jacques Barzun

ECHOES AND REFLECTIONS:
voices of students and teachers

The real authors of this book are the students, teachers, school psychologists and other school staff who have been and are currently living in the confining world of an education structure that has contributed to suppressing the creativity of both student and teacher.

It must be said that there are schools in this country who have managed to provide comprehensive education in spite of the rising number of mandates for testing that limits time for teaching. It speaks to the resiliency of the human spirit to rally above the obstacles to achieve a purpose through much hard work and commitment.

There *are* dedicated teachers, principals and upper level administrators who understand the changing needs of students and have been able to create approaches to instruction that support the independence of self-discovery. They need to be honored and applauded for their perseverance and ability to provide an environment that promotes learning. Although they would not define themselves as such, they are the heroes of this education dilemma we find ourselves in.

We offer some words from students of various ages, teachers with a range of years in teaching, and others in the education field that have contributed to providing quality education and meaningful instruction.. We asked them to sum up their personal experience in their schooling and teaching. We also asked them to cite both positive and negative practices. We spoke to a great number of people and the following collective voices seem to sum up the prevailing perspective of American education.

Students Reflections:

Michael, 5th grade, Tempe, Arizona

Why do we need all these tests?
We are all separate people, not just a group of kids.
More time to ask questions when I do not understand the work.

Rebecca, high school sophomore, Camillus, New York

I am a visual learner; we need more hands-on activities, like science lab.
Student's opinions do not count, no one is ever brave enough to raise their hand and ask, "Why do I need to know this?"
We are expected to learn a subject from the many hours of homework because teachers do not have time to teach the subject because of preparing for tests.
Students should be able to choose classes that could have an effect on future careers, instead of having so many required courses.

Angela, Boston, Massachusetts (on K-12)

Allow for more creative innovation instead of rote memorization.
More development of basic logic and thinking skills.
We need more teachers that love their subject and inspire us to be better students.
Offer more choices of subjects that are relevant to my life.

Katheryn, graduate student, Durham, North Carolina (on high school)

It was hard for me to become interested in subjects that were presented in purely lecture and note-taking style. It could have been presented better in a more engaging way, such as discussion, debates, thought exercises and hands-on practice where you get to see what you are learning about in action.
What we were learning in high school was largely dictated by state exams.
I'm sure that I studied events in history and other subjects, etc. that were irrelevant to me. Historical events can be interesting if presented with the views and interests of the people involved, why the event occurred, explain and explore the outcomes and how it impacts our lives today.
In my school many teachers did listen to our opinions. We were also taught to respect the

opinions of others. What was very helpful was when a teacher would ask about our beliefs on a certain issue and then assign us to the opposite viewpoint to consider a different perspective.

Kevin, high school senior, Hendersonville, Tennessee

I have been fortunate that I attend one of the premier public schools in Tennessee. The material taught to me was of good quality, but it was not always presented in a way that was helpful for me to understand the lesson.

There is not enough substance to history courses. There should be more time spent on studying more closely the causes and effects of historical events, like wars and the reasons that led to the end of many civilizations. Only after we understand why these events happened can we avoid them. It is not enough to simply know that they happened.

Open discussion is essential. It encourages independent thought, a skill that most students today do not even know they possess. It feeds the mind with multiple theories, hypotheses and perspectives. To question and be questioned by one's peers evokes one of the highest processes of thought. Open discussion was part of many of my classes.

Mentors should be a consistent presence in a child's education.

Eugene, Brooklyn, New York (on middle and high school)

Busy work assignments that were given out just so there would be an assignment, did not work for me.

Unfairly graded subjective work like getting a low grade in an art class when you have put forth a lot of effort and felt happy about your creation is discouraging.

Student's opinions were not listened to, which is very important because if you realize early in life that your opinion isn't listened to, you may stop having an opinion.

I do not feel that any of my classes helped me with choosing a career; many of the skills taught were pretty useless. Imagination and pattern recognition are both important skills.

Dolores R. Card, Hermon R. Card

Teacher Reflections:

Lenore, suburban elementary school 22 Years of teaching in traditional classrooms, reading assessment, special education (retired)

There is a prevailing sense of even more responsibility for elementary teachers as they are with their students the entire day. They also teach all aspects of the core curriculum, leaving little time for attending to other tasks such as lesson preparation.

A practice that is not helpful to assess either the progress or decline of an entire student population is that special education students are required to take the mandatory tests and their scores are counted in the final computation. This results in a subjective measurement for success.

I am grateful for the continuous validation and support of both my colleagues and administrators in my building. This kind of environment is essential for creating an atmosphere of confidence and caring for both students and teachers.

Carmen, suburban high school, 26th year of teaching

There has been a great shift in how education is viewed. Teachers in the past were subject experts and responsible for giving students the tools to become lifelong learners whose curiosity, creativity and becoming effective members of society would only increase with time.

We have to teach to the test and a lot of curriculum is lost; time taken away for testing limits how much of the subject is covered.

I need to comply with being assessed as excellent in what I do according to the latest definitions and requirements to keep my job. I do not let it affect my teaching; I continue to practice what I have come to know through experience and caring.

Teachers need heart, passion and caring for their profession, along with support and respect from the administration and the community. Collaboration with other teachers in their respective areas would also be most beneficial, as well.

Maryann, 7 years teaching in middle school, rural school district

Students do not take away detailed information from instruction, teachers need more time to thoroughly cover subjects.

More collaboration with colleges would help students to consider high school courses.

Administrators in my district are very supportive. I feel fortunate, as some of my colleagues in other districts are not having the same experience.

Karen, 25 years teaching in a suburban school district

Through the years I have observed that the curriculum content has been watered down, become easier, perhaps to be able to pass the tests?

It seems that more and more teachers have become negative and are in a defensive mode.

I do not let the assessment of teacher performance assessments affect the way I teach, but if I were a new teacher, it would.

There should be more flexibility in formulating curriculum. Teachers are being forced to all teach the exact same curriculum in the same way. No room for creativity and teaching beyond the subject.

Ted, 34 years teaching English in a suburban district

As an English teacher for thirty-four years, I found the most legitimate and authentic measurement of student learning was arrived at through observing them actually using the core skills. This involved creating situations where they could demonstrate their knowledge and mastery of the skills of reading, writing, listening, thinking and speaking about topics of their own in which they felt a real stake.

Elizabeth, 10 years teaching in a suburban high school

School districts have been lowering standards so that all students are successful, which means that the stronger students are not being challenged.

Teachers instruct so that students show success on tests, not long-term knowledge. Unfortunately it leads to students who only want to pass the test and move on—not learn.

My performance evaluation is affected by how many students pass the state exams.

Elaine, 20 years teaching special education, rural elementary school, retired

Too much teacher assessment. It takes away time from actual teaching, plus there is no additional help for the teacher.

Many teachers do not feel adequate to meet the increasingly high expectations.

What is needed for teaching? Passion, passion, passion and more passion! Being extremely flexible with students through understanding where students are coming from intellectually, physically and emotionally.

Stefanie, school psychologist, 8 years in urban high school, 9 years in district's pre-K program

We are not giving students the opportunity to explore subjects, question ideas and make their own interpretations. We are so test driven that we stifle the students' thought processes and they become rote learners, rather than independent thinkers.

If we think we are helping students by finding ways to give them the answers on tests in order to raise their scores, think again. What will their future be like when they find that they don't have the ability to learn on their own?

Emily, music teacher, middle school, 4 years,

Music in education is an integral part of growing up. It allows students to be part of something larger than themselves. Students learn to understand the basics of music and the musical language; but more than that, students learn to develop self-confidence and diligence.

They also learn to work together to create something beautiful and meaningful as individuals, as a collective ensemble and as a community in their schools.

All agreed that we need to move in a different direction in our thinking about ways we acquire and maintain knowledge. Sweeping changes are necessary to eliminate restrictive methods of teaching and learning in order to provide our current students, and those to follow, with inclusive, all encompassing forms of education.

These are the voices we need to hear and heed.

ENDING THOUGHTS...

Education is about people, not numbers. Education is how we create our communities, our societies, our civilizations. It is how we create our individual lives and how we become whole human beings.

The energy of the Earth is shifting. We are deeply engaged in creating a new civilization. One in which we are all connected, not just by technology, but connected as companions on the journey of living life on this planet.

We have all had a part in creating our current quality of life. Although we, as a people, have made tremendous progress in gaining knowledge and expertise, we have been remiss in our responsibility to recognize and accept the core that is hidden behind the facade that we use as a means of expression about who we are.

That essence is our spiritual nature. The most vital qualities of our spiritual character are the ability to unite with each other and to explore our deepest values.

We have the opportunity, through attending to our current students and new teachers, in a way that utilizes their amazing talents and skills to become the pathfinders and catalysts for this evolutionary change in the human race.

We are all reflections of those who raised us, inspired us, guided us and educated us. What we impart to this generation they will use to bring forth and influence those who follow.

Strength of character is the means by which we accomplish our goals. Spiritual courage is how we maintain peace in our lives. We are accountable to make sure that we send our children into the future with both.

Every life is important—make every life count.

Whatever mystery this changing is, it may be reached through a living teacher, through a doorway of humbling human experience, or through an invisible presence, a companion known only to you. There are as many ways through the opening of this transformation as there are human beings.

The Necessary Pain of Changing
Rumi

FOR KENDRA

July 13, 1997

THE DREAM

You saw me in a field of wildflowers,
running on strong, able legs,
dressed in gossamer garments.
Turning, twirling in my new found freedom.

I will play and laugh and shout out loud,
"I can!" "I can!"
There are so many things to see.
I can't wait for the sunset

I wonder if I can paint and have a dog?
All I can imagine is forever possible.
Unconfined, unconstrained, unencumbered,
I will run, until I fall laughing in the meadow.

For Kendra: Who Rides the Whales and Lives Among the Stars
Dolores Card 1997

ENDNOTES

Chapter 1

1. P.M.H Atwater, L.H.D., 2012, *Children of the Fifth World: A Guide to the Coming Changes in Human Consciousness*, Bear & Company, Rochester, Vermont
2. Gardner, Howard, 1983, *Frames of Mind*, Basicbooks, New York, New York
3. www.litteracyworks.org/mi/home/html
4. David Wright, 2009, *Mathematics and Music*, (*Mathematical World*, vol.28), American Mathematical Society, Providence, RI
5. Laurent Mottron, MD, PHD, 2011, *Nature, International Journal of Science*, Nov. 2, 2011, Volume 479, Issue 731, Riviere-des-Praries Hospital, Montreal, Canada, media contact: w.raillant-clark@umontreal.ca

Chapter 2

1. Bob Dylan, 1964, *The Times, They Are A-Changin'*, Columbia Studios, New York, New York
2. Bob Dylan, 1975, *Tangled Up in Blue*, Columbia Studios, New York, New York
3. John Lennon, 1971, *Imagine*, Abbey Road Studios, London, Ascot Sound Studios, Surry, U.K., Record Plant, New York, New York

Chapter 3

1. Tobin Hart, P.H.D., 2003, *The Secret Spiritual World of Children*, New World Library, Novato, CA
2. Thomas Merton, 1979, *Merton Collected Essays*, volume 12, page 466, *Love and Living*, article (essay) DS, Thomas Merton Center at Bellarmine University, Louisville, Kentucky

Chapter 5

1. Hermon Card. 1998, *The Poetry of Teaching*, Thornetree Hill Poetry Press, Syracuse, NY
2. Hermon Card. 2006,...*or else it's only a job.*, Thornetree Hill Poetry Press, Syracuse, NY

Chapter 7

1. Emmanuel Kant, 2010 (1st edition 1781), *Critique of Pure Reason*, translated by J.M.D. Meiklejohn, web edition published by ebooks@adelaide, The Pennsylvania State University, State College, Pennsylvania, Penn State Electronic Classics Series Publication
2. Alexander Koyre, Nov. 1968, *Metaphysics and Measurements*, vol.162 no. 3853, p. 80, translated by R.E.W. Madison, Harvard university Press, Cambridge, MA.
3. Dr. David Hull, The Metaphysics of Evolution, 1989, British Journal for the History of Science 3, pp. 309-337.

Chapter 8

1. William Blake, *Rouze up, O You Men of the New Age!*, biography, 1983, Poetry Foundation, Chicago, Ill. http://www.poetryfoundation.org/bio/william-blake
2. Andrew Janiak, *Newton's Philosophy*, The Stanford Encyclopedia of Philosophy (winter, 2009 edition), Edward N. Zalta (ed), http://platostanfordedu/archives/win2009/entries/newton-philosophy/

Chapter 9

1. Emma Dickenson, 2011, *Body —conscious Shakespeare: Sensory Disturbances in Troubled Characters*, British Medical Journal, BMA House, London, edickenson@bmjgroup.com
2. University of California-Los Angeles, July 16, 2008, *Mechanics Behind Mind-Body Connection Discovered*, Science Daily.

3. *The Chronicle of Higher Education,* August 20, 2012, P.A37, http://www.umas.edu/religeous_affairs/meditation/

Chapter 11

1. Dr. Gregory Berns, *Why Do People Follow the Crowd,* Emory University, Atlanta, Georgia, ABC Primetime, Jan. 12, 2006, http://abcnews.go.com/primetime/health
2. Eagles, *Already Gone,* 1974, Album, *On the Border,* Asylum Records, West Hollywood, CA

Chapter 12

1. C.W. Leadbeater, 1927, *The Chakras,* Theosophical Publishing House, Adyar, Madras, India, Wheaton, Illinois, USA, London, England, www.questbooks.net
2. Judith Anodea, PH.D., 1987, revised 1999, *Wheels of Light: A Users Guide to the Chakra System,* Llewellyn Publications, division of Llewellyn Worldwide, Ltd., Woodbury, MN. www.llewellyn.com

Chapter 14

1. John Locke, 1693, *Some Thoughts Concerning Education,* sections 161-17, printed for A. and F. Churchill, Black Swan Paternofter-row, London, England
2. R.R. Donnelly, 2008, *The Early Years Framework,* The Scottish Government, Edinburgh, Scotland, http://www.scotland.gov.uk/Resource/Doc/257007/0076309.pdf
3. W.S. Barnett, 2008, *Preschool Education and Its Lasting Effects: Research and Policy Implications.* Boulder and Tempe: Education and the Public Interest Center and Education Policy research unit. Retrieved 2013 from http://epicpolicy.org/publication/preschool-education

BIBLIOGRAPHY/RECOMMENDED READING

Anodea, Judith, PH.D, 1987, revised 1999, *Wheels of Life: A Users Guide to the Chakra System*, Llewellyn Publications, division of Llewellyn Worldwide, Ltd., Woodbury, MN

Atwater, P.M.H. 2012, *Children of the Fifth World: A Guide to the Coming Changes in Human Consciousness*, Bear & Company, Rochester, Vermont

Atwater, P.M.H., L.H.D., 2005, Beyond the Indigo Children, Bear & Company, Rochester, Vermont

Card, Dolores R., 1998, *For Kendra: Who Rides the Whales and Lives Among the Stars*, Thornetree Hill Poetry Press, Syracuse, New York

Card, Hermon R., 1998, *The Poetry of Teaching*, Thorntree Hill Poetry press, Syracuse, New York

Card, Hermon R., 2006,...*or else it's only a job. More Poetry of Teaching*, Thornetree Hill Poetry Press, Syracuse, New York

Hart, Tobin, PH.D, 2003, *The Secret Spiritual World of Children*, New World Library, Novato, CA.

Healy, Jane, PH.D, 1990, *Endangered Minds*, Simon and Schuster, Inc. New York, New York

Luk, A.D.K., Law of Life and Teachings, book I, II, III, 1973, reprint 1975, 2012, A.D.K. Luk Publications, Cincinnati, Ohio, cincinnati@alohapeace.

Silverman, Linda Kregar, PHD, 2002, *Upside–down Brilliance, the Visual Spatial Learner*, Deleon Publishing, Inc. Glendale, CO.

THE AUTHORS

Herm Card is a retired English Teacher from the Marcellus, New York, Central School District.

He is a former baseball player and coach at Syracuse University, NCAA baseball umpire and an education consultant to the National Baseball Hall of Fame and Museum in Cooperstown, New York.

His background in education is extensive—32 years of classroom teaching, along with over 20 years of professional development consulting and motivational speaking. He is well versed in the state of education today, and has written extensively on the topic as education columnist for the Eagle Newspapers.

He has received numerous awards and grants for his teaching, innovative classroom programs, poetry and photography. He is a New York State Educator of Excellence, and his Celebration of Poetry program was named a New York State English Council Program of Excellence.

He has published three books of his poetry and has credits for numerous articles, poetry and photography in education journals throughout the country, and received a cover photography award from the National Council of Teachers of English.

He served 10 years each on the boards of New York State English Council and the Central New York Teacher Center. He is a former editor of *The English Record*, the professional journal of the New York State English Council.

For five years he served as a consultant with CTB-McGraw Hill and the New York State Education Department on the development, evaluation, implementation and scoring of the current series of New York State ELA assessment tests, and authored Barron's New York State Grade 5 Test Preparation Manual.

Despite the textbook irony of those last associations, he is an activist for the cause of minimizing the burden of assessment testing and government in education, in the quest to return teaching to teachers.

THE AUTHORS

Dolores Card has taught metaphysical principles and doctrines through classes, seminars and workshops as well as Reiki practitioner certification for 25 years. She is a Reiki Master, ecumenical minister and spiritual advisor.

She worked as a core subject tutor with special education students for twelve years at the elementary and middle school levels. Even then, she could see the negative effects of mislabeling unique abilities as deficiencies.

As Director of the Syracuse University Rape Center she founded ICASA, the International Intercollegiate Coalition Against Sexual Assault as well as implementing relationship violence prevention programs across the United States, Ireland, England and Wales.

She acted as New York State's primary trainer of police agencies and medical personnel on protocols for medical/legal intervention with victims of sexual assault.

Prior to working at Syracuse University, she provided direct services to child victims of sexual assault and incest for 15 years at the city of Syracuse's Rape Crisis Center. She also administered and supervised school-based prevention education programs, K-12, reaching over 30,000 students a year.

She has been interviewed on numerous TV programs and newscasts, including CNN, National Public Radio and the BBC and authored numerous articles in magazines and journals. She has been a keynote speaker at national and international conferences throughout her career.

In 2002 she testified before the United States Congress regarding date rape drugs and in London, England, was a catalyst in the founding of *Femnet*, the International Violence Against Women website, an interactive informational, resource for advocating for women's rights.

Her professional awards include: Eleanor Roosevelt award for rape prevention programs, New York State Governor's award for crime prevention and Crime Prevention Practitioner of the Year, awarded by the New York State Crime Prevention Coalition, a Citation from the New York State Senate in honor of her contributions to crime prevention.

She loves to travel, and loves dogs, her family, cooking, shopping and the New York Yankees.

Herm and Dolores live in Syracuse, New York, with their 16 year old Border Collie, Molly Rose, a new kid of the animal kingdom.

CPSIA information can be obtained at www.ICGtesting.com
Printed in the USA
BVOW07s0829260813

329446BV00001B/6/P